The
Total
Cost
of
Poverty:

(In the United States)

The Total Cost of Poverty:

(In the United States)

A Conservative
Argument for
Greater Economic
Equality

V. Earl Berg

iUniverse, Inc.
New York Lincoln Shanghai

The Total Cost of Poverty: (In the United States)
A Conservative Argument for Greater Economic Equality

iUniverse, Inc.

For information address:
iUniverse
2021 Pine Lake Road, Suite 100
Lincoln, NE 68512
www.iuniverse.com

ISBN: 0-595-31948-3

Printed in the United States of America

For—
My dear and patient wife, Leigh;
for my precious children, Andrea and Emily.

Contents

Acknowledgements

I must start with my parents. They toiled on an Iowa farm that my brother and I might have a better life and the best education.

My enduring wife, Leigh, has been kind and tolerant throughout this project. Although she purchased a gun, not once, to my knowledge, did she actually chamber a bullet.

The University of Washington faculty both taught and inspired. Special thanks to Drs. Hubert Locke, Robert Halvorsen, Robert Plotnick, Patrick Dobel, Richard Zerbe and Alan Rabinowitz. I think often of your good natures and good minds, in that order.

Special thanks also to Mark Long and Dr. Kenneth Stikkers, friends and seers, always with better ideas than mine and encouraging words when most needed.

Finally, thanks to my editors, Wayne Ude, Marian Blue, and Jack Botts. Their guidance on this little book's structure and their notice of my bad grammar and usage was so thorough that I have only myself to blame for any deficiencies that remain.

Earl Berg

Prologue: My Politics

The first thing readers demand to know about a social or economic tract is the political bias of its writer. Any claim of objectivity is met with thin smiles, if not snickering. The information age is partly to blame. Pundits Right and Left have now achieved the once fantastic possibility of proving any proposition, in the affirmative or negative, on any question, absolutely and conclusively, using multiple studies. Their determinations on all matters are suspiciously consistent with their biases. Such ingenuous behavior tars all social commentators, not merely those of us who deserve it.

So who am I? Raised on an Iowa farm, I emerged with the typical Midwestern work ethic, pigheaded self-sufficiency and distrust of authority. After college, I worked in industry for three years and owned a small manufacturing business for five years. In my early career, I worked as an area campaign director for U.S. Representative John Y. McCollister from Nebraska (a Republican, second district), and as a legislative aide for Nebraska state Senator Vard Johnson (a Republican, eighth district). However, I am by training an academic. I have taught political science and economics for fifteen years at colleges in Nebraska and Washington state. After teaching, I decided to try my hand at this little book.

On almost all matters of political principle I am a conservative, but on matters of program, my conservative friends view me with deep suspicion. I do not fear government action as much as they do, and in some matters I insist upon it. Because I am not a thoroughgoing conservative or thoroughgoing liberal, both sides view me as vacillating or ornery; some dislike me merely for the warm sensation it gives them.

I would state my conservative credentials in this way: I regard personal freedom as the foundation of a vital personal life, vital society and vital economy. I demand the broadest range of freedom that human foibles and failings will permit. I believe in generous rewards for merit, for personal responsibility, initiative, inventiveness, competence, energy, community service, and most importantly, for fulfilling one's duty to family. I regard work, kept in balance with a zeal for life's joys, as a societal obligation, as well as a virtual guarantor of upward economic mobility. I hold Equal Protection Under Law and Equal Opportunity for

All as sacred precepts of legitimate governance. I believe that the most estimable justice rests upon personal character—our empathic capacity, our ethics, our sense of duty and compassion—not upon behavior enforced under law.

These precepts command my allegiance because they insist upon individual empowerment and responsibility, and a fair chance for everyone.

But I part company here with many of my conservative friends. When I say everyone, I mean everyone. Giving every child a fair and competitive chance in life requires that every family controls approximately equal resources to safeguard the development of their children. I insist that every parent have the financial capacity to pay for healthcare for their children, to educate and socialize their children, to provide a decent home. I insist that every individual and family have the financial capacity to save for emergencies such as disease, injury and bouts of unemployment, and to save for retirement.

I observe that some people do not have the mental or physical ability to economically produce at a level that commands enough income to meet the full cost of living. Yet parents need to be able to meet their family financial responsibilities regardless of their capacity to command an adequate wage in the labor market.

Freedom does, in the main and over time, promote justice, but freedom also tends to favor the strong. I see government as a legitimate arbiter and intervener between the interests of the strong and the weak, between the favored and disfavored.

Ideologically, you must make of me what you will.

1

Overview

My object in this thin book is to paint on one canvas a picture of the total social and dollar-cost of poverty and inequality.

I hope to convince you:

That all U.S. citizens who work full-time need and deserve to make enough income to meet their needs, to fulfill their reasonable wants and to live in health and dignity. All parents must also earn enough to meet their family financial responsibilities. Fulfilling child-rearing responsibilities in a modern society—responsibilities that we rightly demand of every parent—requires substantial cash outlays and savings.

That poverty's consequences permeate our society. Poverty makes a mockery of the sacred principles of our nation. Poverty corrupts the principles and the practical functioning of representative democracy. It undermines equal voice, equal protection under law, equal opportunity for all, and humankind's universal need for safety and fulfillment and some measure of happiness. Poverty creates the reality and the perception of victimization, exclusion, disenfranchisement. It creates hopelessness, desperation, bitterness, fear and all manner of bad values and bad behavior. It leads to lawlessness, riot and war. It exacerbates terrorism. Poverty poisons our personal souls whether we are rich or poor.

That sustained or severe or chronic poverty always weakens and sometimes fatally corrupts almost all social relationships. This includes parent/child relationships, male/female relationships, employer/employee relationships, police/community relationships, politician/citizen relationships. Poverty breeds suspicion of, and disrespect for, adult and institutional authority.

That poverty fosters resentment in all quarters. The poor are embittered by their exclusion from common opportunities and experiences; the middle class feels squeezed by marginal incomes and taxes; the rich believe they are taxed excessively and that government wastes their dollars on welfare and "transfer" programs. The poor generally construe the rich as oppressors; the rich generally construe the poor as slackers. The poor resent government for its intrusive and stigmatizing administration of welfare; the rich resent government for taking and, as they often see it, misusing their tax dollars.

That poverty corrupts courtship and destroys families. That repeated episodes of unemployment and inadequate wages weaken the confidence of young men and women that they can be successful economic players and successful family providers. For this reason many young men and women shun family and parental responsibility.

That when a critical mass of impoverished people are pressed together geographically into a low rent district (a ghetto or barrio), a "poverty culture" arises. This culture validates and perpetuates its own worldviews and myths and lore and rights of passage and codes of conduct. These values and behaviors loop back upon themselves: poverty causing crime, crime causing poverty; poverty causing family breakdown, family breakdown causing poverty. These circular cause/effect associations perpetuate poverty and pass the hurtful, antisocial behaviors of the poverty culture on to the next generation.

That when individuals and parents are able to take care of themselves and their children, through respectful work at comfortable and dignified rates of pay, a great many of our social problems will be ameliorated.

That when our nation reduces poverty, or more precisely, the horrific array of antisocial and criminal and sociopathic behaviors that come with it, the size of government can also be amply reduced.

That the antisocial and sociopathic behaviors fostered by poverty and family breakdown cost our nation, quite literally, trillions in public and private dollars every year. These costs represent massive and unnecessary macroeconomic inefficiencies. These economic losses are cumulative and largely irretrievable.

Finally, I want to convince you that reducing poverty and inequality represents a Magnificent Convergence of liberal and conservative ideals. Conservatives want, in part, more personal responsibility, more personal empowerment, and less government; liberals want, in part, a fairer income and wealth distribution. I suggest that more income and more responsibility will come hand in hand. Middle-class incomes generally create middle-class wants and values and behaviors. Permit me also to point out that the number of persons who are financially struggling are in the tens of millions and increasing. An enormous electoral advantage awaits the political party that can articulate and deliver a practical program to significantly broaden opportunity and prosperity.

> [All of the statistics cited below, and many more, are attributed to their sources in Appendix Two: Statistics on Poverty and Inequality: Current Levels and Historical Trends.]

In 2003, about 35 million Americans fell below the poverty line.

Among poor persons, 45 percent are white, 26 percent are black, 25 percent Hispanic. Children under 18 represent 34 percent of the poor. Almost 10 percent of the elderly are poor even after receiving Social Security. Were there no Social Security, 49 percent of the elderly would fall below the poverty line.

There were 7.3 million poor *families* in 2003. Among poor families, 75 percent have children. Female-headed families represent 50 percent of all poor families. To the surprise of many, fully 42 percent of poor families are married-couple families.

The working poor, those working full-time but with incomes below the poverty line, are estimated to number between 10 and 15 million.

Income inequality has sharply increased over the last thirty years. Various inequality indexes put the increase between 17 and 48 percent from 1975 to 2003. The bottom four-fifths of all households—that is, the lowest-income 80 percent of all households—lost income share during this period. The highest-income 20 percent had a 17 percent increase in share; the top 5 percent realized a 38 percent increase in share; and the top 1 percent had a 100 percent increase in share.

The lowest-income 40 percent of households commands only 12.5 percent of total U.S. household income. The top 5 percent controls 22 percent of all household income.

In 2003, the average CEO of the nation's one thousand largest corporations made about 10 million dollars. That is about 1000 times more than a minimum wage worker makes and about 400 times the pay of the average worker.

Had the minimum wage risen at the same rate as executive pay since 1990, the minimum wage would now be about $22.00 per hour, as opposed to the 2003 federal minimum wage of $5.15 per hour.

Had the minimum wage risen at the same rate as executive pay since 1975, it would now be about $41.00 per hour.

In fact, however, since the minimum wage reached its real-dollar high in 1968, it has lost 36 percent of its value when adjusted for inflation.

Income inequality is as nothing compared to wealth inequality. The wealthiest 1 percent controls about 33 percent of the nation's private net worth. The bottom 40 percent controls only .3 percent (3/10ths of 1 percent) of the nation's private net worth. In 1998, before recession drove down the value of financial assets, the wealthiest 1 percent controlled 38.1 percent of all private net worth. For what it is worth, in 1929 the concentration of wealth in the hands of the top 1 percent was estimated to be between 45 and 49 percent.

The wealthiest 1 percent of families controls about 100 times the *combined* net worth of the bottom 40 percent. The bottom 25 percent of families have, on average, zero net worth. That is correct: on average, zero net worth. The bottom 40 percent have an average net worth of $5,500. The top 10 percent of families have an average net worth of just under $3 million.

The total dollar-cost of poverty is horrendous. I estimate this cost to be at least 2 trillion dollars per year in 2003 dollars. (Chapter ten itemizes these costs.) With all true and justifiable opportunity costs included, the figure is closer to 3 trillion dollars per year. Putting the cost at 2 trillion dollars, that is about $6,960 for every man, woman and child in the United States. That is about $14,500 paid out every year by every working person. Two trillion dollars is roughly 17 percent of U.S. gross domestic product (2003). All of this cost cannot, of course, be eliminated; some poverty will always persist, and some public welfare assistance will always be needed. But these costs can be reduced in loose proportion to our ability to reduce poverty.

This annual 2 to 3 trillion dollar-cost represents massive systemic inefficiencies. These losses are cumulative. To give perspective, it has been estimated that the military component of the Afghanistan and Iraq campaigns may cost the United States $100 billion. Just one year's economic losses to poverty are 20 to 30 times that amount.

The causes of poverty are at once complex and simple. Complex because many factors determine the capacity of an individual to get and to keep the job that can keep him or her out of poverty. Differing intellectual capacity, differing emotional and mental stability, differing physical abilities, a criminal record or a spotty employment history all affect individual earning capacity. Some spiritual and artistic personalities cannot or will not readily comply with the demands of commercialism, leading to voluntary and involuntary poverty. Improper, or merely different, socialization can lead to employment problems. Problems with speech, usage, grammar, dialect, dress, posture and mannerisms can cause trouble at job interviews and with interpersonal relationships on the job.

And then there is discrimination—racial, gender, ethnic, aesthetic.

Macroeconomic factors also contribute to poverty. Economic growth (and the geographic distribution of the work that is created) must be such that all new-comers to the labor force can be absorbed. Another cause of poverty is supply/demand imbalance in the labor market: when too many or too few people are educated or trained in a profession or trade. These supply/demand mis-matches can take years for a full-employment equilibrium to reestablish itself. Recessions can sometimes lead to long-term poverty and always create short-term poverty for millions of individuals. Globalization—trade, outsourcing, moving factories to cheap-labor nations, sudden insertions and extractions of capital—is worsening poverty in all but a few nations, despite globalization's promise of long-term benefits.

There is, however, an overarching *distributive* cause of poverty. Every payday there is A Great Dividing Up of the total national income among our citizens. Who gets how much is determined by the relative power of individuals to deter-mine the size of the slice they take from the total economic pie. On any given payday, this is a zero-sum game: if some take more, others get less. The rich, the strong, the shrewd, the aggressive, by way of their economic power and advan-tage, and by way of the political power that economic power can buy, are able to take and hold for themselves a huge over-share of our national income and national wealth. At the present, near-record extremity of inequality, what is left of the national income—to be divided among everyone else—is simply not enough to fulfill the needs and reasonable wants of the rest of the citizenry.

The simplicity of poverty is this: poverty is ended with a stable, well-paying job. Note that there are three components to that proposition. First, there must be a job. Second, it must pay sufficiently. Third, over one's lifetime, one's income must be stable enough that his or her family is able save for the inevitable crises a family faces (injuries, illnesses, bouts of unemployment) and to invest for the children's education and for retirement.

What might be done?

I do not intend, here or later, to argue to the last detail for a particular pro-gram. But I do feel obliged to point constructively and hopefully in a general direction.

My general proposition, put brashly, is to eliminate both the super rich and the super poor. One way or another, more income must be gotten into the hands of our lowest-wage workers. The centerpiece of my scheme is the minimum wage. The minimum wage is a familiar and simple tool, but one with profound ramifications if it is allowed to lag, or if it is raised too high, without responding to the consequences. I will recommend a new form of minimum wage.

For a higher minimum wage to mean anything to a specific worker, that worker must have a job. Free market capitalism, if nothing else, has proven to be a powerful growth model. Sufficient growth will occur if recessions can be kept short or avoided. The business cycle has proven to be an obstinate conundrum for economists. I will recommend a different approach to recession avoidance and management.

Raising the minimum wage enough to comfortably support a family will create labor cost pressures on businesses and create international trade competitiveness problems. Part of the trade issue is the head-to-head competition between American workers and cheap foreign labor. Neither the average American business nor the average American worker can win this competition against globalization and cheap foreign labor; the wage-rate differentials are too great, and there are multitudes of desperate workers waiting in line for jobs. This head-to-head competition between developed nations and developing nations must be moderated in kind and pace; it is creating havoc on all sides. I will recommend some new terms for international trade.

Raising the minimum wage will push the cost of almost all goods up. Worker/consumers will have to pay more for products and services and they will not like it. A gain-nothing, inflationary spiral at first appears inevitable. There are, however, large, countervailing savings that will come into play automatically and quickly when the minimum wage is raised to the levels I will recommend. These savings, regrettably, will not fully offset price increases in the short term. Various challenges will arise. I will attempt to explain the economics and politics of these challenges in a later chapter and offer some possible answers.

Raising the minimum wage will reduce the numbers of the super poor, but the money to pay for the higher minimum wage will not automatically or necessarily be drawn from the incomes of the super rich. Whatever approach is used, that approach must assure that the income and wealth that is redistributed to the poor comes from the rich, not from the middle class. I will suggest a framework for this redistribution.

This nation is facing a practical and moral reckoning. We must answer this question: are we or are we not going to structure our economy so that all of our adult workers can earn a sufficient wage to purchase the needs and reasonable wants of their families?

There is some urgency. The costs of poverty are piling upon us at an alarming rate at a moment when our nation faces a sea change in its economic demographics as the baby boomers retire.

Because the costs of inequality and poverty are so large, the national economic surplus that our nation might have invested in schools and universities and infrastructure must now, instead, be spent on poverty—on welfare and police and prisons and child protective services and much more.

And what are we spending? A great deal of it is borrowed money. The United States has so far (February, 2004) accumulated $7.13 trillion in national debt ($51,700 for every person currently working), and $6 trillion more in non-funded Social Security obligations that will fall due by 2038 (another $43,500 for every person currently working). New actuarial data has just revealed that without new taxes Medicare will be insolvent by 2019, eight years ahead of estimates made just last year, and long before baby boomer retirement peaks. These debt obligations will be payable by our children and grandchildren, robbing them of their capacity to pay their immediate public and personal expenses, and markedly limiting their capacity to save for their own and for their children's futures.

Modern multinational corporatism has become so large, so fast-moving, so sophisticated in achieving its objects of growth and profit, so able to caress and coerce political leaders for the public policies it desires, that democratic governance, with its innate tentativeness and inertia, has lost its capacity to guide the direction and pace of economic expansion.

The pace of this change and the character of this change are destabilizing many national cultures, including our own. The hugely imbalanced wage competition between American workers and cheap foreign labor—which is inextricably linked to importing and outsourcing and moving U.S. corporations overseas—is steadily pushing the lowest-income 40 percent of worker/consumers onto subsistence wages.

Globalization is creating large-scale workforce dislocations, and the concurrent cultural shocks. It is widening the have/have-not gap almost everywhere. Governmental power (and government's sluggishness) has been overrun by corporate power and speed. Corporate power cannot be granted supremacy over governmental power. It is the prime directive of public governance to safeguard the public destiny. Public governance must take the throttle of this runaway train of corporatism—especially in the realm of international trade.

The increasing mal-distribution of income and wealth evident over the past thirty years cannot continue without devastating effects on both small and medium-sized American businesses, and on the purchasing power of American worker/consumers. The dream of many businesspersons of an army of low-wage workers cannot but end in a nightmare for most businesses and workers, and for the nation. An army of low-wage workers is an army of cash-poor consumers and cash-poor families. As the prosperity of the American consumer goes, as the prosperity of the American family goes, so will go the prosperity of American businesses. And, as well, the stability and peace of our nation.

[Permit me to mention again that additional statistics on poverty and inequality, and their source attributions, are in Appendix Two.]

2

Poverty and Personal and Family Responsibility

Personal and family and social responsibility require more than keeping one's nose clean before the law and keeping one's pants up or skirt down. Personal and family responsibilities are, to large degree, financial responsibilities.

Any conscientious parent knows the sobering—no, the terrifying—financial injunction upon them. It means providing healthy and sufficient food, warm and respectable clothing, and decent housing; it means paying for health insurance and deductibles and co-pays and most prescriptions; it means providing educational and developmental opportunities for the children—soccer, softball, swimming lessons, theater, dance, art classes, trips to the zoo. It means providing reliable and safe transportation, quality daycare, good pre-schools. It means paying for birthday and Christmas presents, occasional meals out, video rentals, and on and on.

Meeting family financial obligations also means that the parents must protect their earning power—their professional or vocational standing. It means parents must be able to save money for continuing education, or perhaps reeducation or retraining if a new career track is necessary. It means parents must be able to save for emergencies—serious injuries, serious disease, bouts of unemployment. Parents need to be able to save prudently for retirement as well as for an occasional vacation.

Saving is essential for family risk management and income protection. Most people want to save, but unstable work and insufficient wages make saving almost impossible. The typical lower middle class or poor family saves up a few hundred bucks and then the car breaks down or one of the kids gets sick. There is always something: illnesses, injuries, auto repairs, appliance repairs, home repairs, school clothes, birthdays, Christmas. The chronically poor are locked in a hope-crushing cycle of pulling together a few bucks, and then having to spend to the last dollar to hold life and limb together.

When the rules of the economic game deny a man or woman or family suffi-cient income to meet these responsibilities, their socialization, and the socializa-tion of their children into the common experience and values of the mainstream culture, are threatened. (This is not an unqualified endorsement of the values of the middle class; it is, however, a qualified endorsement of the values of the mid-dle class as contrasted to those prevailing in the underculture.)

Nor is "sufficient income" just about needs. Individuals and parents deserve the modest prosperity that allows them to buy the occasional small and fanciful things that make life worth living at all.

Poverty, Sexual Responsibility, Courtship and Marriage

How can we persuade teens and young adults to postpone sexual gratification, or at the very least to rigorously guard against pregnancy, until they are emotionally stable and in a solid, and preferably a marital, relationship? Permit me to con-struct a proximate answer.

Young men or women, supported by loving parents in a financially-secure home, with positive adolescent work experiences and good prospects, with a little cash in their pockets and hope in their hearts, will be far less likely to act self-destructively, that is, beyond the pale of adolescent misjudgment and experimen-tation. Young men or women who see meaningful and viable opportunities spread before them will generally not forsake these opportunities for unprotected sex. For those lucky youth who have love and prosperity at hand, the opportunity costs of casual or careless sex are apparent. There will be greater caution in the aggregate, even though not heeded in each instance.

A young woman, firm in her self-respect, who earnestly believes that she can make her dreams come true by force of her own effort, within in a society that will give her a good education and a fair chance to do so, will be less likely to truncate her dignity and freedom and dreams through dangerous, self-abasing promiscuity. She will be much more likely to guard against pregnancy.

A young man who is confident in his financial ability to meet his obligations as a family provider and protector, and who has had his conscience formed by ethical mentoring and caring relationships, will be less inclined to walk away from his children—or at least less inclined to walk away from his financial responsibilities to them. When a young man is humiliated by his inability to provide even for himself, the last thing he is willing to do is assume the financial obligations of marriage and children.

Not wanting marriage and children does not mean that he does not want sex. We might like to lecture: Abstain! But the forces at work are, in every way, potent. The stupidities of youth, and human weakness at all ages, will always be with us—the yielding to hormones, the youthful experimentation, the parties, the beer, the drugs, the sex, the unintended pregnancy. We cannot stop these things without crushing the very humanity out of us. However, the stupidities and experimentations of youthful passage do not irreparably warp the values and behaviors of adolescents who have around them a loving family, a caring community, and a social order that meets their economic needs and validates their own value and the value of others.

A person must also feel self-assured before interpersonal commitments come freely. A young man must feel confident in his potential; he must feel that he has prospects, especially economic prospects. Family providership, particularly providership by the male, is a powerful cultural measure of the cut of the man. Failing to be able to provide for either one's own needs or those of one's family can be a stinging humiliation. It can be taken by the young man as a self-indictment against his basic worth, or he can see it as an indictment against the world for what he believes it has done to him. When things fall apart, the first resort of the failed father may be verbal abuse against the spouse and kids, and against himself as well. A second resort is to opiates of relief and gratification—often alcohol or drugs or promiscuous sex. A third resort is to a desperate search for alternative means of exercising personal power, occasionally progressing to physical abuse within the family, or criminality.

Financially-strapped parents can make for a dangerous home. The lack of money can create a marital relationship that swings between low-grade, irritating, petty conflicts over bus money, and knock-down-drag-outs over why the old man or old lady can't get a better job. All too often it ends in child and spousal abuse. (Data on child and spousal abuse are in Poverty and Antisocial and Criminal Behavior chapter.)

Sometimes the father's first act, and sometimes his final act, is to flee responsibility. Dad leaves. Often, given his paroxysms of domestic violence, it is fortunate that he does. Be that as it may, mom and the kids are left to live on her income and, very likely, public assistance.

Relentless money pressures—or recurring pressures from which there seems no hope of escape—crush the spirit and undermine comfort and respect in marriage and courtship.

The Statistical Link Between Poverty, Single Parenthood, Unwed Motherhood, Teen Motherhood and Family Abandonment by the Father

Patrick Fagan and Stephanie Coontz[1] examined Census Bureau data on income and family structure. They found that: "Among our very poor families, those with incomes less than $17,200 per year, marriage has all but disappeared, and among working-class families with incomes between $17,200 and $34,300[2] a year, married parents don't exist for 45 percent of the children."

In 2003, fully 34 percent of all births were to unmarried women. In the 1950s the number was 5 percent. Using race as a proxy variable for poverty is also revealing: in 2003, 28.5 percent of white infants were born to unmarried women and 68.2 percent of black infants were born to unmarried women.[3]

(An extremely hopeful development is that teen births have dropped significantly. From 1991 through 2003 the African American teen birth rate decreased by almost 50 percent, and by 30 percent for the overall population. This corresponds in time with increased funding for high school sex education, increased availability of sexual counseling, dramatic welfare reforms, and a long economic expansion, with historically low unemployment. The relative contribution of these factors to lower teen pregnancy rates is not clear.)

The most disturbing dynamic of poverty is its circular relationship with family breakdown: poverty exacerbates the breakdown of family; family breakdown exacerbates poverty.

The increase in poverty rates associated with illegitimacy and family abandonment by the father or mother is enormous. Single mothers are nine times more likely to live in severe poverty (less than 50 percent of the official poverty line) than are married mothers.[4]

Maggie Gallagher, in her book *The Abolition of Marriage*, citing data from the National Center for Children in Poverty, noted that a child born out of wedlock is 30 times more likely to live in poverty at some time during his childhood than is a child born to a married couple that remains married throughout the child-rearing years.

The combination of living in a single-parent family and living in poverty renders children twice as likely to drop out of school, 2.5 times as likely to become out-of-wedlock teen parents, and 1.4 times more likely to experience chronic unemployment.[5]

Census Bureau data reveal that when parents divorce, the resulting household wherein the child resides (almost always with the mother) is twice as likely to drop into poverty than before the marital split. When a father leaves a family (divorce or non-marital abandonment), the resulting household wherein the child resides (again, usually the mother's household) experiences a drop in income, on average, of 26 percent.[6] When a non-poor family divorces, the household that contains the children suffers, on average, a 50 percent drop in income.[7]

Children living with never-married parents are eight times more likely to grow up below the poverty line. (Ben Wattenberg, "Welfare as Seen by Those Who Know," American Enterprise Institute, August, 1996.)

I do not want to wear you thin with statistics. The relationships between poverty and teen births, births to unmarried women, family abandonment by fathers, and single parenthood have been studied beyond anyone's patience with the subject. One conclusion is consistent: poverty increases single parenthood, and single parenthood raises the likelihood of the family unit being in poverty by a factor of from seven to ten times, depending on the study one reads.

3

The Dollar-cost of Meeting Family Financial Responsibilities

To approximate the cost of raising a family in a lower-middle-class lifestyle in modern society, we must know what belongs in this market basket, and what these things cost. Knowing the true cost of living, our duty then is to structure the economic rules of the game such that families can meet these financial responsibilities.

We need to know how much income is needed to cover the full cost of getting our kids successfully launched into the world, and ourselves (the parents) through retirement and into our graves with a smidgen of dignity and a little cash to pass on.

Please remember that we are not talking about a minimum or subsistence income; we want to identify an income sufficient to assure the positive development of our kids, of the next generation. A necessary part of healthy child development is to assure some security and happiness for the parents; frustrated, angry parents are seldom good parents.

It is helpful to personalize the question. Using your own sense of responsibility, what market basket of needs and reasonable wants and education and developmental opportunities and emergency savings and retirement savings do you want for your family? To a considerable degree we must insist upon the same educational and socialization experiences for the children of other families that we want for our own children.

The dollar-cost of the goods and services needed to safeguard the health and development of all members of a family is substantial. Not only must a family buy for the here and now, but responsibility and prudence require saving for future crises and needs.

There is no such thing as a universally-applicable, basic family income. Too many factors are at play. Some families have one child, others four or five. Neither is it possible or desirable that every person's earnings follow the same locked-step, upward progression over his or her life span. People want different things of life. Not everyone wants to work full-time all the time. Many students must work part-time, and many seniors want to work only part-time. Artists and authors frequently choose to work part-time—sometimes at a cost only to themselves, sometimes at terrible cost to their families.

Many moms and dads prefer to take time off from work to be with the kids. And all families are not two parents and two kids; single parent families are a common and permanent part of our culture. As well, many people believe it is beneficial if one of the parents is at home with the kids, instead of working.

A viable economic framework must accommodate differing lifestyles, fluid circumstances, and excursions in and out of the workforce. Despite such differing needs and wants, we simply must start somewhere. There is no choice but to generalize and to average across these varying needs and wants. As a practical matter, let us focus on the typical family of four—mom and dad and two kids—and assume that both parents are going to work.

Very well. How much income must a family of four in the United States earn to meet its financial responsibilities? How much income for immediate needs? How much for needs that loom in the future—buying a home, the children's education and the parent's retirement? How much income is needed to save prudently for family crises—unemployment, illness, injury? We want to identify a conservative, self-reliant income for this family, without extravagance.

Economists use many approaches to put a value on this. The U.S. Department of Agriculture has, for example, constructed a Thrifty Meal Plan, listing categories of food and their cost as a basis for the official poverty line. The USDA also estimates the cost of raising children based on a market basket of goods and services. The U.S. Bureau of Labor Statistics tabulates the average annual expenditures for various income groups. This is an "actual expenditures" measure; it is inclusive of a broad range of typical family purchases. The U.S Bureau of Economic Analysis compiles the Personal Consumption Expenditures Tables, and data on average actual personal savings. Localized cost-of-living surveys are also popular.

A notable survey of the cost of living was commissioned by the Maryland State Organizing Project for Family Economic Self-sufficiency. (Dr. Diana Pearce and Jennifer Brooks, "The Self-sufficiency Standard for the Washington, D.C., Metropolitan Area," funded by the State Organizing Project for Family Economic Self-sufficiency, 1999.)

Pearce and Brooks describe their survey as a "basic needs" estimate. It might be fairly characterized as a "minimal, comfortable, self-sufficiency" income estimate. Four additional family cost components will be added: the income needed to support savings for family emergencies, savings for the children's college education or training, and savings for retirement. A small allowance for vacation and recreation was also added. The Pearce/Brooks values are adjusted to 2003 dollars.

[This survey considers important urban/rural cost differences, utilizes actual on-site market-basket costing; includes a definition of family that is preferred for this purpose (two adults, one preschool child and one school-age child); specifies a conservative housing size (one bedroom for adults, one bedroom shared by the children); bases the cost of housing on surveyed fair market rental averages; utilizes the USDA Low Cost Food Plan which is 25 percent more generous (and more realistic) than the USDA Thrifty Food Plan; bases urban transportation costs on the use of public transit only, and bases suburban/rural transport on the cost of operating an eight-year-old car; assumes that one-third of the family's health care premium is covered by an employer (co-pays, drugs, and dental to be paid by the family); includes a modest 10 percent allowance for miscellaneous, and adjusts for federal and state taxes. This survey reflects selected counties in the Washington, D.C. area. This suburban/semi-rural area is used, in part, because it represents below-national-average consumer prices—an index of 96 for the cited county. [Prince George's County, MD; Suburban/Rural Washington, D.C., bedroom community; Cost-of-living Index—Selected Metropolitan Areas; Office of Management and Budget; (national average = 100; low = 86; high = 240; this area, Baltimore, MD = 96).] Values have been adjusted to 2003 dollars, rounded to hundreds. All items were adjusted by the CPI-U index except for health care. Health care was inflated at 4.7 percent per annum, the actual rate for this period.]

PEARCE/BROOKS COST-OF-LIVING ITEMIZATION AND PRICING:

Housing	$9,500
Child care	12,100
Food	6,700
Transportation	3,500
Health care	3,100
Household operations	3,500
Taxes added back (21%)	9,700
Child care credit	-0-
Universal child tax credit (2 kids)	1000

Pearce/Brooks "Self-sufficiency" income: $49,100

Plus add-ons to support savings needs (annual set-asides)

Children's education savings: $4,200
(Two children; $5000 per year of college, for four years of college, per child. Saving from birth to age nineteen; inflation = 3 percent; return on investments = 7 percent)

Retirement savings: $6,000
($25,000 per spouse; $50,000 per couple(in 2003 dollars); forty-year accumulation; inflation at 3 percent; return on investments = 7 percent)

Risk management savings (emergency savings): $2,000

Vacation/recreation add-on: $2,000
(Assumes a one-week vacation @ $1000; three one-weekend outings @ $200 each, totaling $600. total; and $400 for all other recreation for two adults and two children for one year.)

Total wealth-accumulation (savings) need:	$14,200	$14,200

**Total, approximate, lower-middle income requirement
for a family of four, before taxes:**   **$63,300**
(cost of living index = 96; 2003 dollars)

Inferred Income per Spouse: **$31,650**

**Implicit Wage per Hour, Assuming
Full-time Work (excluding value of
employer's health insurance
contribution):**   **$15.83** per hour

These are conservative criteria. Few couples can consistently contribute to a college fund starting from the moment of birth of their children. The education fund, at $5000 per year per child for four years of college, covers about half the cost of an average state university's tuition. (It is assumed that the son or daughter will pay the rest through work and loans.) Most couples cannot contribute to a pension fund continuously for forty years even at the low level indicated. Only about one-fourth of all workers have health insurance for which employers pay 66 percent of the premium, as assumed here. The emergency fund, at $2000 per annum, is less than is needed to cover the average annual medical deductibles and co-pays for two adults and two kids.

It should be said that the approximate lower-middle-income requirement for a family of four, defined above as $63,300, does not mean that a kid just out of college needs to be immediately hired on at this rate. It means that $63,300 is the approximate amount of income needed per year during the child-rearing years. The family income might, for example, start with the young couple, together, making $40,000, and at the end of twenty years making perhaps $80,000 (in

2003 dollars). In this example, savings accumulation for retirement will continue for another twenty years (a forty-year accumulation period).

Another approach used to estimate a family's full-cost-of-living income needs is to take the USDA poverty line and add in actual, average expenditures for child care, health insurance, wealth accumulation needs, emergency saving, recreation and taxes. This income estimate comes to $57,800.

Another method is to use the Bureau of Labor Statistics' Average Annual Expenditures for Consumer Units. (The four person consumer unit is a rough proxy for the family of four.) This figure comes to $52,700.

Another often-used measure for defining a lower-middle-income is simply multiplying the USDA poverty line by 3. This method is popular among economists because it is quick and historically quite accurate. This yields a figure of $55,900.

These estimates range from $52,700 to $63,300. The average is $57,450.

The short of it is this: it costs roughly $57,000 per year during the child-rearing years to provide for a family of four in the United States in 2003 dollars. That is about $28,500 per adult earner, or $14.25 per hour, with both parents working full-time. If we happen to think that either mom or dad should spend more time at home, then the other parent needs to earn more.

We have a decision to make regarding the fundamental structure of our economy: do we pay people enough to meet their family responsibilities through stable work at sufficient wages, or, do we pay people low wages and then subsidize them with welfare and transfer payments just up to the poverty line, thereby perpetuating poverty, the underculture, and all the destructive values and behaviors and social costs that follow?

When couples have children, they need sufficient income whether they are conscientious or irresponsible, smart or stupid, productive or laggards. If the parents are stupid or ignorant or indolent or irresponsible or unproductive, we must consider the cost to ourselves and to our nation of condemning their children to live in poverty during their developmental years, and very likely during their adulthood. We must not punish the next generation because we do not like the character or marginal productivity of their mothers or fathers. Nor should we shortchange the future of our nation.

As a matter of cold economic efficiency, we should not tolerate an economic structure that condemns generation upon generation of kids to poverty, even if we have nothing but contempt for the poor generally.

Every family with children has a roughly-identifiable range of immediate income needs and a roughly-identifiable range of lifetime income needs. In a "free" social and economic system we cannot guarantee everyone an income precisely matched to these needs. The best we can do is to set a minimum wage below which no adult with children should fall and then do all we can to be sure that work is available.

Getting income into the hands of families, through work at sufficient wages, and letting families make their own fiscal decisions, is almost always better for the family—and greatly more efficient for the overall economy—than administering hundreds of public assistance programs.

There is a moral component to all this: people have a right to the dignity of being able to take care of themselves and their children. They have a right to the modest empowerment that adequate income gives them. It is a significant bonus for society that personal financial empowerment inherently applies pressure upon the individual or family to exercise greater financial responsibility.

The conditions that make family formation (marriage) a viable option for a young man or woman, and the conditions that reduce the prospect of family dissolution, are grounded to large degree upon family financial stability and comfort. A family may survive severe or sustained or chronic poverty, but the development of the children, on the broad averages, will not fare well. And neither will we when their dysfunction comes to visit us.

4

Poverty and Antisocial and Criminal Behavior

A link between poverty and crime has always been known. Crime is heavily concentrated in poor urban areas, perpetrated by the poor against the poor.

Author George Winslow summarized it this way:

> "…simply take a map of a major American city and put a red
> dot wherever a homicide [or almost any category of street crime,
> for that matter] occurred. Soon small red lakes start forming in
> the city's poorest neighborhoods."

A 1998 survey by the New York City Police Department found that just twelve of the city's seventy-four precincts—all twelve located in the impoverished areas of Harlem, the Bronx and Brooklyn—reported 46 percent of the city's 1,960 total murders. The twelve most prosperous precincts reported only 2 percent of this total.

Race can be used as a proxy variable for poverty. For blacks, unemployment rates are typically twice as high, and poverty rates three times as high, as for the overall population. Blacks comprise 30 percent of federal prison inmates and 46 percent of state inmates, while comprising 12 percent of the population—a curiously similar ratio, again, of about three-to-one.

If the racial crime rate is adjusted to reflect white and black populations in "extreme poverty" (below 50 percent of the poverty line), the crime rates between whites and non-whites are similar for every age level.[1]

Studies[2] have consistently found that poverty is positively associated with the homicide and property crime rate.

It is not categorically true, but it is substantially true that our prisons are filled with poor people. It was even more so before the war on drugs put many middle-class, recreational drug users and prosperous drug dealers behind bars. One can conclude that either the poor are in fact committing more crimes, or that the judicial system, for any given crime, is sending the poor to prison with disproportionate frequency. It is, of course, both.

Poverty Exacerbates Crime; Crime exacerbates Poverty

High crime rates drive businesses out of neighborhoods, taking the jobs with them. New business investment is frightened away from the communities that need the investment most. Business and home owners in crime-plagued areas are reluctant to make property improvements. This reluctance to invest soon degrades the appearance of the community, reduces property values and undermines community pride and spirit. When property values decline, owners disinvest. Potential buyers and mortgage institutions shun the degraded property and neighborhood. The businesses that do stay are forced to charge higher prices to cover losses from theft, to pay for extra private security and to pay higher property damage and theft insurance premiums.

Crime-ridden neighborhoods are avoided by customers who might otherwise do business in that neighborhood. Fear generally impairs freedom of movement in "bad" neighborhoods, hence impairing economic freedom.

Unemployment and Crime

Unemployment (vs. poverty) has a more complex statistical relationship to crime. About half the studies using aggregate unemployment rate data (that is, including all ages, all races and both sexes) show a statistically-mixed association between unemployment and crime. However, criminals are overwhelmingly young men sixteen to twenty-five years of age. For this age group, unemployment rates and crime rates significantly correlate for both property and violent crimes.

Unemployment and property crime are consistently linked for all FBI index property crimes, whether in the aggregate or for each separate type of property crime.[3]

It has long been known that dropping out of high school is closely linked with future difficulties finding and holding employment. Between 60 and 70 percent of incarcerated men have not graduated from high school. Graduation from high school, which increases a persons employment stability, also dramatically reduces criminal participation, by as much as 60 percent for nineteen-year-olds.[4]

The relationship between employment and crime is circular. Once an individual gets a criminal record, his or her employability is reduced. This is referred to as *scarring* or stigmatizing. Scarring can lead to the repeated rejection of former criminals in their search for work. Former criminals keenly feel a potential employer's wariness. They often transmute their resentment towards a specific employer into a generalized resentment for society, leading to a broader array of antisocial behavior.[5]

About 70 percent of state prisoners are employed at the time of their arrest.[6] This has been cited to reinforce the position that a strong majority of arrestees are employed, implying a weak link between employment and crime. However, when stated negatively, that about 30 percent of arrestees are unemployed, the truer meaning of the statistic is clear: 30 percent is about five times the average unemployment rate for whites, and over double the typical unemployment rate for blacks. Further, of the 70 percent of prisoners who were employed at the time of their arrest, over two-thirds worked only part-time.

Several studies[7] confirm the most convincing statistic: approximately 5 percent of employed persons engage in crime, compared to 16 percent of unemployed persons. In other words, the criminal participation rate for unemployed persons is three times greater than for employed persons.

Income Inequality and Crime

The association between income inequality and crime is less intuitive. Whereas unemployment or divorce or an unplanned birth can throw a family or individual into immediate financial and emotional crisis, inequality has less direct connection. Its effects, at first glance, seem distant from the immediate financial motives of criminals. Few criminals, particularly young criminals, understand how income and wealth inequality translate into their personal position in the income and wealth hierarchy. They simply compare their possessions to those of others or to their own wish list.

Keeping up with one's peers is a powerful sentiment. Adolescents in particular want to keep up with their peers. Stories of homicides and beatings over tennis shoes are anecdotal anomalies, but reflect the power of "coolness," ownership and relative social position among young adults. Corporate marketers are obsessed with defining cool, raising youth's consciousness to ownership, and creating status-based product demand.

The term *demand* is apt. Our ego demands to possess whatever confirms the image our ego holds as good. Self-worth, in both the adolescent and adult mind, is often measured by ownership. Our image and wants are largely referenced to what others around us have. Again, the young are especially susceptible. Not "having" can be a humiliation. It is one thing to view one's position as: "I don't have this or that because I choose to spend my money in other ways, and I will buy it later when I am better off." It is quite another to see one's position as: "I can't have this because I am broke and no matter how hard I try, the world is going to kick me back to the ground." For the male, if the desired possession is a symbol of manhood, not having it is an affront to his manhood. For the materially-focused individual, having transcends the object. It is to be strong or weak, cool or not cool, successful or deficient, victim or victor, competent or incompetent, able to provide for self and family or not able to provide. Having or not having can be seen as winner or loser. Having or not having relative to those around us is immediately evident to us even if the link to academic notions of inequality is not.

Poverty, Family Breakdown, and Crime

Statistically, family breakdown is significantly associated with poverty, delinquency and crime. About 70 percent of juvenile delinquents in state institutions come from single-parent families or were raised by a caretaker other than their natural parents.[8] About 75 percent of adolescent murderers come from single-parent families.[9]

A black child from a single-parent home is more than twice as likely to engage in criminal activities as a black child from a two-parent home.[10]

Cynthia Harper and Sara McLanahan, in a paper published by the American Sociological Association, tracked the developmental history of 6,400 boys over a span of twenty years. They found that children who grew up without their biological father in the home were roughly three times more likely to commit a crime that led to incarceration.[11]

Child and adolescent development in poor households is at the center of delinquency and crime. Research has consistently found that, on average, low-income parents are less nurturing to their children, less complimentary to them, quicker and more belittling in their criticism, more likely to use inconsistent and harsh discipline, and less likely to supervise their children closely when compared to higher-income parents.[12] Eight studies over the last seventeen years (all of the studies reviewed) found a significant link between poor parental supervision, erratic and harsh parental discipline, weak parent-child bonding and subsequent juvenile and adult crime.[13]

The Crimes of Child Abuse and Intimate Partner Abuse

Poverty correlates strongly to the criminal acts of child abuse and neglect, and child abuse and neglect correlates strongly to future crimes committed by the abused children.

The heinousness of the worst abuse is beyond comprehension. Beatings with fists and whips are standard fare. Torture, injection with addictive drugs, forced drunkenness, starvation, solitary confinement in darkness, sex acts of every form and with every conceivable partner (human and animal), are all in the court records.

In the United States, about two-thousand children die annually from child abuse and neglect—six per day.[14] A longitudinal survey from 1980 through 1993 showed a 149 percent increase across all categories of abuse (physical, sexual, emotional and neglect).[15] On a hopeful note, the passage, in 1996, of several child abuse prevention measures has resulted in a 23 percent aggregate decrease in all forms of abuse through 2002. In 2003, approximately twelve out of every 1000 children (1.2 percent) in the United States are victims of substantiated abuse. Victimization rates range from about 4.4 per 1000 children for Asians (Asian children victims compared to all Asian children), to 25.2 per 1000 children for African Americans (African American children victims compared to all African American children). There were one million confirmed cases out of three million reported cases. A great deal of child abuse goes undiscovered or unreported.

Child abuse and neglect strongly correlate to single-parent households, unemployment, and high family stress.[16]

A 1993 study found that the rate of child abuse is lowest in intact, married families. Child abuse was six times higher in "blended" families (stepmothers/stepfathers), thirteen times higher in single-mother families (than in married families), and twenty times higher in single-father families. The risk of child abuse was twenty times higher if the true biological parents were cohabiting, rather than married.

By far the most dangerous place for a mother or a child is in a household where the mother and her boyfriend are cohabiting. That rate was thirty-three times higher than the rate for married couples.[17]

In a longitudinal study (NIS-3, ending in 1993) families with incomes over $38,000 had the lowest incidence of abuse; for families with incomes between $19,000 and $38,000 the incidence was ten times higher; for families with incomes below $19,000, the incidence was twenty-two times higher. (Dollar values have been updated to 2003 equivalents.)

Studies[2] over the last thirty years have consistently found that the higher the unemployment rate for any group of families, or the lower the family income for any group of families, the higher the rate is for child abuse for that group.[18]

We have looked at the relationship between poverty and the crime of child abuse. What about the relationship between child abuse and future crime by the abused child?

Child abuse and neglect strongly associate with future criminal propensity. Peter C. Kratcoski[19] found that 26 percent of juveniles convicted of murder had been abused. Of fourteen juveniles convicted of murders so heinous that juries condemned them to death, twelve had been brutally abused as children; five had been sodomized by family members.[20] When offenders self-described their parent or caretaker relationship, between 50 and 70 percent professed to having been abused as children.[21]

A study by the National Institute for Justice found that about 38 percent of violent crime can be associated back through family history with child abuse or neglect, and that abused children could be associated forward to approximately a 60 percent increase in subsequent violent crime.[22]

Poverty, Intimate-Partner Abuse and Violence Against Women

Perhaps you have guessed: intimate-partner violence correlates to poverty. Although evident in every social class, abuse is most common and most deadly in the underculture. As with child abuse, intimate-partner abuse has disastrous intergenerational consequences.

In 2003, between 800,000 and 4,000,000 women (depending on the definition of abuse) within the general population were physically abused by their husbands, live-in partners, or boyfriends.[23] Of all females murdered in the U. S., about 30 percent are slain by their husbands or boyfriends.[24]

For the general population of women, between 1 and 12 percent experience one incident of intimate-partner violence in the course of the year of the particular survey.[25] (Again, this broad range, from 1 to 12 percent, has to do with how abuse is defined, who is included in the sampled population, and differing methods of data collection.)

The rate of incidence for intimate-partner abuse in aggregate, that is, for the overall population and occurring in the last twelve months, is approximately 6 percent.

Contrast the above *general population* incidence of intimate partner abuse to that for low-income women:

In a 1997 Massachusetts survey of 734 AFDC recipients, 19.7 percent of women with a current intimate partner reported current physical abuse by that partner. In their "lifetime," 64.9 percent had experienced partner abuse.[26]

(Current abuse is defined as within the preceding twelve months. *Lifetime* abuse is typically defined as within the last five years or as happening anytime during one's adult life. Physical abuse in this survey was defined as being hit, slapped, kicked, thrown, shoved, attacked with a weapon, hurt enough to go to a doctor or forced into sexual activity.)

A Passaic County, New Jersey, survey of 846 welfare recipients found that 19.6 percent reported current abuse; 57.3 percent reported intimate-partner abuse as adults.[27]

A study by Saloman, Bassuk and Brooks[28] of 436 homeless and publicly-housed women, 409 of them receiving some form of welfare assistance, reported that 60 percent experienced "severe" lifetime physical violence (slapped at least six times, kicked, bitten, hit with fist, hit with object, severely beaten up) by an intimate partner. "Current" abuse was reported by 32.4 percent.

In the same study, 82 percent of homeless, long-term (over five years) welfare recipients had experienced lifetime domestic violence.

In a random survey in Chicago of low-income women—1/3 on welfare, 2/3 not—33.8 percent of welfare recipients, and 25.5 percent of non-recipients had experienced "severe aggression" (beatings, rapes, attack with a weapon).[29]

In a survey of Washington state welfare recipients by Raphael and Tolman,[30] 60 percent reported either physical or sexual abuse as adults. For a group of Chicago women in a welfare-to-work program, 58 percent reported partner abuse within the preceding twelve months.

Tolman and Raphael in a 2000 "Review of Research on Welfare and Domestic Violence"[31] summarized the results of twenty studies from 1996 through 2000. They reported that the rate of lifetime domestic violence among women on welfare ranged from 34 to 65 percent, with most between 50 and 60 percent.

"Recent" or "current" rates ranged from 8 to 33 percent, with most between 20 and 30 percent.

Unemployed men are twice as likely to "severely" abuse their partners than men working full-time. Domestic violence rates are 5 times higher among females below the poverty line.[32] The typical abuser is currently unemployed or has a history of chronic unemployment.[33]

The Bureau of Judicial Statistics, in a May 2000 report, found that women living in households with the lowest annual income (less than $8,000 in 2003 dollars) suffered abuse from intimate partners at a rate 7 times higher than for women living in households with the highest annual income ($80,000 and over in this study, 2003 dollars).[34]

Intimate-partner violence is evident in all economic classes, but its incidence dramatically increases with poverty. The rise in incidence is in near-perfect proportion to decreases in income.

A woman's financial resources can be lifesaving. In a Texas study, only 16 percent of women who had their own sources of income or savings returned to relationships with their batterers after exiting battered women's shelters.[35]

There is, as well, a substantial level of women's violence against men—inflicted primarily in revenge for their partner's abuse. Females typically compensate for relative physical weakness with weapons.

The intergenerational effects are devastating. A child's exposure to the father abusing the mother is the strongest risk factor so far identified for transmitting violent behavior from one generation to the next.[36]

The Overarching Causal Dynamics of Crime

In our materially abundant nation, very little crime arises from abject need. Crime arises most fundamentally from disrespect for self, others and the social structure. It arises when violent methods of problem resolution are modeled by parents and peers and media to children and adolescents.

Crime arises when positive channels of personal power are economically choked off, and spiritual channels of power are not evident. It arises when the lack of financial power is compensated for by thrill-seeking, drugs, sexual conquest, gang alliances and any other mechanism the poor can find to bring direction (however misguided),belonging (however corrupt),and vitality (however destructive) to their lives. It arises when families and communities do not love and nurture their young men and women.

Most crime has its roots in the circular, mutually-exacerbating relationship between poverty/inequality/unemployment/low wages on one hand, and on the other hand, the family breakdown that follows.

These circular, reinforcing relationships magnify the effect of poverty. Poverty aggravates family breakdown; family breakdown aggravates poverty. Poverty exacerbates crime; crime exacerbates poverty. Poverty and family breakdown create the values and behaviors of the underculture; the values and behavior of the underculture create poverty and family breakdown. Bad values create bad behavior; bad behavior creates bad values.

A Word about Violence, Crime, and the Media

The link between the media and violence and crime has little to do with poverty. I include these paragraphs because many of my liberal friends dismiss media influence as a red herring argument thrown up by conservatives to draw attention away from poverty and inequality. TV and film—the visual media—however, has an especially powerful influence on less-read and less-discerning individuals, who are found in disproportionate numbers in the underculture. The media is a coconspirator with poverty in the formation of values and behavior.

Those who believe that the values and behaviors portrayed in the media do not alter real-life behavior (that a heavy diet of violence and sex does not create a model and an appetite for violence and sex in some persons), need open their eyes to the research and to the world around them. TV, film, books, periodicals can either nurture and enlighten us, or debase and delude us. They exert powerful influences upon our values and behavior.

Homo sapiens are the most imitative species on earth. We are all constantly looking for and absorbing models of behavior. Less consciously, we absorb the values that underlie those behaviors. The young, particularly, are analyzing their world to know how to act. No one is immune. Pugnacious free-thinkers are always looking around to see what other free-thinkers are thinking.

Media models behavior and infers values. At the moment of this writing, the United States is in the midst of a War on Terrorism following destruction of the World Trade Center towers on September 11, 2001. In the weeks following the twin towers attack, other bomb threats were prolific. After a few mosques were vandalized and the stories aired on national news, there were just under 1000 copycat attacks during the first two weeks following September 11.

Some creative terrorist(s), in follow up, decided to send out anthrax-laced letters to government officials. Within two weeks, dozens of twisted individuals sent powder-laced letters to scare hell out of whomever they hated. Hundreds more called their local police or media to threaten attacks with anthrax or smallpox. One sociopath alone sent out over 900 threats. An angry middle-school youth guns down his classmates in their school; within three months there were at least six multiple murders in other schools around our country, and at least two dozen threats by students to commit murder in their schools. The killings and threats are perpetrated by angry teens (very few of them poor, I should add, but bitter for their own reasons) who suddenly had presented to them a dramatic model of how to channel their anger.

Perhaps you remember the arsenic poisoning of encapsulated Tylenol. Almost instantly after the first episode, other similarly-poisoned bottles of Tylenol began showing up in dozens of other stores, along with the poisoning of other products which lent themselves to tampering. One person does it; then dozens of others do it; then hundreds threaten to do it. Perhaps you remember the syringes-in-Coke-cans episode. The examples are truly endless. Our court records are full of such copycat episodes.

These examples refer to TV news coverage, but realistic drama works similarly. When television and film solve disputes with fists and guns, a model for problem solving and manhood is being presented to the viewer. When heroes are doing the punching and shooting, not only is a model being presented, it is being lionized. In TV and film, rogue behavior, physical retribution and vigilantism are presented as models of strong, independent action; that is, heroic action. These themes resonate with victim mentalities and the criminally-inclined.

Freedom of our media is a sacred value, yet we must acknowledge human tendencies and vulnerabilities, especially regarding the malleability of our children, and the vulnerability of those who are less intellectually discerning. It is outside of my purpose to argue the case for or against media influence. Again, the media is a coconspirator with poverty in forming so many of the hurtful values and behaviors evident in the poverty culture and the underculture.

The criminal activities I have highlighted represent but a fraction of the antisocial behavior that poverty provokes. I have not discussed drug and alcohol abuse, needle-transferred HIV infection, babies exposed to crack cocaine, runaway and abducted children, astronomical school dropout rates, gang formation and much more. Nor have I raised the specter of the wholesale riots and insurrections over poverty and civil rights that punctuate this nation's history and periodically smash and burn down entire neighborhoods in our cities.

I must quit or you will become impatient with me.

5

Poverty and Health

The poverty-inequality-health relationship has been fiercely studied. There are studies within countries and between countries; within and between states, counties, localities and census tracts; in aggregate and case-by-case comparisons; using objective and subjective health assessments, referencing every disease, using every methodology, and employing every measure of poverty and inequality known to woman or man.

The relationship between poverty and health is at once simple and complex. Complex because there are many variables and intricate linkages; simple because the truth, as surely as physicians and social scientists can claim any truth about anything, is that poverty and inequality are bad for everyone's health, ending in tens of thousands of premature deaths every year, and adding billions to our national health care costs.

A nation's per capita personal income and wealth, and the degree of economic inequality in a society, are key indicators of individual and family health. Considering nothing else, if the 40 to 45 million uninsured individuals in our country commanded the household income to afford health insurance, our nation's health statistics would be dramatically improved.

Permit me for a moment to paint with a broad brush: poverty exacerbates any disease or condition or injury that is made worse by late diagnosis, or by the failure to diagnose, or by delayed treatment or no treatment. That doesn't leave out many ailments.

Regarding mental health, not only do poverty and extended periods of unemployment correlate significantly to higher incidences of depression, anxiety and other mental illnesses, the stresses of poverty also weaken immune defenses, worsening other *physiological* conditions. Mental stress from personal problems and coping with general dysfunction increase the incidence of unhealthy behaviors, such as smoking, unhealthy eating, lack of exercise, neglect of preventive measures and failure to see a doctor when needed—to say nothing about substance abuse.

The relationship between income and mortality holds true from top to bottom of the income and wealth spectrum: on average, the poorer any population group is, the poorer its health and the higher its mortality rate.

A 1997 study[1] found that the lowest income group had an adult mortality rate 390 percent higher than the rate for the highest income group. The second-to-lowest income group had a mortality rate 59 percent higher than the wealthiest group; the third-to-lowest group a rate 34 percent higher.

A 1998 study[2] compared various metropolitan areas with different average income levels and different levels of income inequality. Looking at differences in inequality only, the "excess mortality" (the morality in excess of the national average mortality rate) was 64.7 deaths (per 100,000 persons per year) for the area with the least income inequality, compared with 95.8 deaths per 100,000 for the area with the highest income inequality. Areas with *both* high levels of income inequality *and* low average income had an excess mortality of 139.8—over double the excess mortality of the low inequality/high income areas. That excess mortality of 139.8 deaths per 100,000 was equivalent to the combined death rates for lung cancer, diabetes, motor vehicle accidents, HIV, suicide and homicide for that year.

People with less income and wealth have higher mortality rates for almost all the most common and the most deadly diseases. [3] [4] [5] [6] Higher mortality correlates to lower income levels, lower wealth and higher levels of inequality within a population. Males who drop out of high school (dropping out of high school strongly correlates to employment problems and poverty) are about twice as likely to die of chronic diseases such as heart disease, and just under twice as likely to die of communicable diseases.

Infant mortality is dramatically and tragically linked to poverty. In 2003, the infant mortality rate for whites was about 5.7 (deaths per 1000 white births). For African Americans, the rate was 14.0, or two and a half times higher than for whites. In 2003, about 33,000 babies died in the United States. It is the unreserved conclusion of several studies[7] that universal access to health care—as that translates into parental education and pre- and post-natal care—accounts almost totally for the higher level of black infant mortality. From the studies cited, between 40 to 60 percent of the infant deaths were judged to be needless.

Women living in families with annual incomes under $10,700 are over three times as likely to die of heart disease, and just under three times as likely to die of diabetes, than are women living in families with incomes over $26,700.[8] (Dollar values from 2000 study have been converted to 2003 dollars.) African Americans have higher death rates than whites from lung, prostrate, breast and colon cancer, heart disease, liver disease, diabetes, AIDS, stroke, injury—not to mention homicide. This difference is linked to unhealthy behaviors disproportionately evident within the poverty culture, not having health insurance and to other health access problems.

Life expectancy is another gross measure of public health. For whites born in 2003, life expectancy is about 77.4 years; for African Americans, 71.7. A white male in the U.S. general population who lives to age fifteen has about a 65 percent chance of reaching age sixty-five; a black male who lives to the age of fifteen in Harlem, New York has only about a 37 percent chance of surviving to age sixty-five.[9]

Another study looked at life expectancy for black and white populations that had reached age sixteen. Poor black males living in urban environments have about a 38 percent chance of surviving to age sixty-five, and about a 7 percent chance of surviving to eighty-five. Affluent whites living in rural areas have about a 90 percent chance of living to sixty-five and a 40 percent chance of living to eighty-five.[10]

In a 1998 study of life expectancy that looked at data for Chicago, white males living in high employment areas outlived African American males residing in high *un*employment areas by 10.16 years. Homicide alone reduced African Americans' life expectancy by 2.56 years; for whites the reduction was negligible—about .28 years (28/100th of one year, or about one day).[11]

Being murdered is particularly hard on one's health. Murder and other crime-related injuries and deaths significantly affect the health statistics of low-income groups. African American males are seven times more likely to be victims of homicide than white males. African American females are just over four times more likely to be victims of homicide than white females.[12] The National Center for Health Statistics reports that the national homicide rate for African American males fifteen to twenty-four years of age is just under ten times as high as for white males in that age group.

As tragic and news-sensational as our nation's current 14,000 annual murders are, the national health consequences of homicide are as nothing compared to national health consequences of the 1.5 million other violent crimes (assaults, robberies, rapes).

As mentioned, the degree of income inequality within a nation or state or locality also affects health care. A 2000 study by Kahn, Wise, Kennedy, and

Kawachi,[13] compared the self-reported health of 8060 women in states with high levels of income inequality to states with low levels of income inequality. Individuals in states with high levels of inequality had a 60 percent greater self-reported rate of depressive symptoms and an 80 percent greater risk of "fair" or "poor" health. Only 2 percent of women in the highest-income fifth of the surveyed group reported fair or poor health, compared with 15 percent of individuals in the lowest income fifth (or 7.5 times the rate reported by women in the wealthiest quintile). A 1998 cross-sectional study found that individuals living in states with the highest inequality were 30 percent more likely to report fair or poor health than those living in states with the lowest inequality. This 30 percent inequality effect is on top of the two-to three-fold higher rate of self-reported mental and physical ill health for low-income individuals.[14]

I cannot take any more of this. I hope you cannot either. I have rattled on for several pages and still have two hundred note cards in front of me. I have not yet presented any health data on the monstrous consequences of child abuse and spousal abuse and violent crime injuries, nor on the mental illness that so disproportionately attends severe or sustained poverty. Nor have I documented the consequences of delayed or foregone visits to the doctor, nor of having a county hospital emergency room serve as one's primary health care provider, nor the consequences of inadequate home heating or cooling or living in vermin-infested housing.

Nor have I detailed the effects of unhealthy behaviors that are so disproportionately evident in the poverty culture and the underculture—smoking, alcohol abuse, drug abuse, comfort eating, promiscuity (and the higher rates of HIV and sexually transmitted diseases that follow). These are seldom behaviors in the discretionary sense; these behaviors typically reflect the grim socialization and modeling prevalent in the streets and in the homes of the ghetto. These behaviors are occasionally driven by physiological or psychological addictions.

My conservative colleagues often demand that the poor "just quit" their bad habits—their smoking, drinking, drugs. However, these behaviors are evident among rich and poor alike. The difference is in the incidence and the extremes. The rich and poor are alike in this way: some can quit, others cannot or will not. It depends a good deal on what is left of one's self-respect and hope and will. It depends on whether the person's functional and moral judgment is intact and whether one's reason is strong enough to overrule one's emotions and impulses.

I have not documented the fear, anger, suffering, death, and dollar-cost of having 40 to 45 million of our citizens without heath insurance—8.5 to 10 million of them children, 21 million of them women, 9 million of them working poor.

Millions more work full- or part-time and earn wages just *above* the poverty line, but are still without health insurance. Indeed, working persons (full- and part-time) and their dependants comprise 85 percent of those without health insurance.

Let me end with a glint of humor. I suggest the following federal legislation to remedy the inequalities in access to health care: no federal or state or local legislator or executive would be permitted to carry health insurance coverage for their children or grandchildren that is not also provided for all other children either through private or public coverage. Nor would these politicians be permitted to pay for any health care for their children out of their own income or wealth. A few weeks of living under the anxiety created by this law will spur swift passage of the health care protection that all children and adults deserve.

Let us call my facetious proposal in the above paragraph Plan A. I suggest (seriously) Plan B: to adjust the rules of the economic game so that all persons have enough income, through work and sufficient wages, to buy their own health insurance and to pay also for those health care costs that are not covered. If enacted, most of the Medicaid program, and many medical payments now under Social Security, would simply disappear from government budgets. Read this as: smaller government, less bureaucratic overhead, more power and choice for individuals and families, more dignity for individuals and families.

The relationship between poverty and health confronts us with a stern moral test. Is one child's life or suffering worth more than another's? Does another parent's child deserve the same medical care that we want and demand for our own child? Should poor parents have to endure the anxiety and occasional terror caused by diagnosis and treatment that come too late? Do we mean what we say when we speak of all God's children and of being created equal and of inalienable human rights and of an equal opportunity for healthy child development? If not in ministering to the health of our children (and adults for that matter), when are we to mean these words?

6

Poverty and the Sacred Principles of Our Nation:

Equal Opportunity for All

Equal opportunity means many things. It means fair treatment in hiring, promotions and layoffs. It means equal pay for equal work. It means equal educational opportunity.

I suggest that most fundamentally equal opportunity means—and requires—substantial equality in the basic, full-cost-of-living income among adults with children.

Equal economic opportunity in any near-perfect form is not possible. Yet we rightly demand it for our children and ourselves. Indeed, equal opportunity is perhaps the chief criteria by which we judge the legitimacy of any law or nation. In the United States we have gone to the trouble of writing equal opportunity into constitutional law. It reflects our belief in the ideal and the right of each person to realize his or her potential.

Perfectly-equal economic opportunity is impossible for many reasons. Some of us are loved, encouraged, consoled, educated, coached; some of us are beaten, insulted, threatened, neglected. Some of us are socialized into meekness, timidity, shame; some of us are socialized into arrogance and aggressiveness. Some of us have our development stifled by bad parents or bad schools. Some of us are pushed by circumstance into emotional imbalance or depression or anger, wile others emerge into adulthood stable and strong. It is not possible nor desirable to standardize our early developmental experiences in the home. We have to trust the parents—an admittedly regrettable state of affairs in some instances.

Our hereditary and socialized natures play a large role in our economic success. Some of us are given by nature to be contemplative or artistic or poetic or spiritual; others are by nature doers and builders and accumulators. Some are disposed by genetics to good health or bad health; some are smart, others not so smart. We reach working age formed by a thousand factors we cannot control and by a thousand others we can control.

However, the "natural" differences between us can be significantly reduced by education and training and socialization. Even the social consequences of differing relative intelligence can be reduced by assuring that each person possesses skills enough, however narrow, to command a rung on the economic ladder. Education and training remain the surest ticket to economic success and mobility into the middle class. Education and training are power, and they are the foundation of our idealized economic meritocracy. But educational opportunities across the United States are grossly unequal.

Families who can afford to buy a superior education for their children cling viciously to that advantage. The rich preserve their advantage in primarily two ways. One is to live in a prosperous neighborhood with a well-funded public school district. The second is to buy their way into private schools. The difference in educational outcomes between rich and poor districts can be dramatic. This difference results not just from school funding levels. A large part of the difference, again, is the culture that so often forms around poverty.

In 2003, more than half of all fourth graders, as well as half of all eighth graders, in urban public schools failed to meet the minimum standards in reading or math or science set by their states. In our poorest districts, just under 50 percent of all students drop out of high school. That is not a typo: just under 50 percent drop out. We might expect this in a Third World country, but this is our country and these are our kids.

The inability of many public schools to deliver a first-class education is the result of persistently second-class public funding and our failure to equalize funding between rich and poor districts and public and private schools. Schools in poor urban neighborhoods lag behind middle-income school districts for at least five reasons. First, because the poverty culture brings its behavioral problems into the schools. Second, because the multi-cultural, multi-language character of most urban, low-income school districts confronts teachers with extremely difficult communication and teaching challenges. Third, many kids raised in the ghetto often have a diminished faith, or belief, in the value of education; they do not see the payoff in the experience of adults around them. Fourth, often the parents do not emotionally support, or cannot intellectually assist, their children. And last, despite all these added problems, the poor districts (supported typically, principally by property taxes) have less money per pupil to deal with their problems.

My conservative colleagues often claim that we cannot solve public education's problems by "throwing money at them." All the while many of these conservatives (and rich liberals as well) throw huge sums of money into the private education of their own children. This "can't-solve-the-problems-by-throwing-money-at-them" is regrettable rhetoric. Anecdotes about bad public schools and wasted money and misguided programs are always abundant, but better funding almost always yields better education. Give public schools twice or three times the per-student tuition rate that these schools now receive, (equivalent to private schools), and let public schools pick the best students and reject the troublesome students (those with language and discipline and performance challenges), and then let us see how relative performance stacks up between the public and private offerings. Every application of reason and ethics would demand that public schools, except for the most prosperous ones, should receive more money per pupil precisely because public schools are compelled to accept every child in their district, regardless of the problems/challenges that child brings to that district.

The U.S. tradition of funding education with property taxes has always had the pernicious result of providing the least money for the most needful districts. Low-income, low-property-value districts have the highest levels of "special needs" and emotionally troubled and delinquency-prone students. To get enough operational revenue, low-property-value districts have to tax their citizens at high rates. Prosperous school districts, with fewer problems, can levy taxes at dramatically lower rates because of the high value of the property.

The per-pupil expenditure disparities between rich and poor public school districts can be enormous. In 2003, the range is from about $5000 per student in Mississippi to over $13,000 in New Jersey. (These values have been adjusted for cost-of-service-delivery differences between the regions.)

And this is not the only disparity. As mentioned, rich districts almost always have much lower property tax *rates*. A broadly representative example is found in Wisconsin. The Gibraltar school district is suburban and wealthy; it spends about $10,000 per student. The Peshtigo district is urban and poor. It spends about $7500 per student. This is after state school district equalization adjustments. Gibraltar's real property, however, is worth much more, requiring a tax levy rate of only $3.16 per $1000 of assessed value to provide a premium education for its kids. *Peshtigo must tax its much-less-affluent citizens $9.91 per $1000 of assessed value to deliver that district's $7500 education. In effect, Peshtigo's much-less-affluent* *citizens must pay three times the tax rate of the richer district to get 25 percent less dollar value in education*

And this is not the end of the matter. Rich districts can raise more private money from prosperous parents and alumni and businesses. These funds are not subject to any school funding equalization formula.

The wealth advantage described above is largely that of the upper middle class over the middle and lower middle class, and of course, over the poor. This advantage relates to *public* schools. However, the rich and super rich typically use private schools.

Private schools are a cherished enclave of advantage for the children of the rich. High tuition fees keep out the troubled and troublesome riffraff. Exclusionary entrance standards and vigilant admission reviews serve to weed out students with poor academic records, as well as students with English language deficits, discipline problems or "special needs." State and federal law prohibits overt race discrimination, but the primary tool of discrimination is the high tuition. Proving overt discrimination in court is difficult, expensive and time-consuming. Most parents walk away from discrimination lawsuits because of the cost and difficulty of proving the case, and of course, because their children must get on with their education immediately: the child's education cannot wait the years it takes for the case to get to the top of a civil court docket.

Vouchers will further benefit the well-off. Vouchers, as currently discussed or implemented, give the parents the per student dollar value the state spends on each child's education, to be spent by the parents on a school of their choice. The problem is that states on average spend $5500 to $7500 per student per year; private school tuition is typically much higher—from about $12,000 to $25,000 and up. The parents must pay the difference out of their own pockets. Only the rich and upper middle class can afford such costs. The poor, who most need better schools, are almost summarily priced out, while the affluent get subsidized to give their kids this educational advantage. Meanwhile, to the extent that students do transfer to private schools, the public schools will be left with an even higher percentage of "special needs" and troubled students, and with less revenue to deal with their problems.

My conservative friends insist that poverty is not the cause of educational inequality. Poverty indeed does not *cause* poor academic performance, just as poverty does not *cause* crime. Poor academic performance has many causes. Behavioral problems or fear caused by gangs and cliques in the schools can poison the educational atmosphere. Problems can follow if the parents are indifferent or hostile to education. Problems grow from the scorn for education shown by peers in the poverty culture or the underculture. Problems follow from defaced and gloomy corridors and classrooms, from playgrounds surrounded by hateful and tawdry graffiti and surrounded by chain link and barbed wire that declare society's indifference towards the children of the poor; from run-down schools that look—to students to teachers to administrators to parents—like failed institutions before anyone even steps in the door. Poor academic performance results from classrooms with thirty to thirty-five students, five of them with abusive or neglectful parents, five more who are abusing drugs or alcohol, five more whose *parents* abuse drugs or alcohol, and ten whose fathers have abandoned them and their families' financial responsibilities. All this taken together can be counted upon to end in poor academic performance, and worse. This is the pervasive dynamics of poverty at work, poisoning the individual and the family and the culture.

Good education requires adequate funding. Equal educational opportunity requires closely balanced per-student funding between rich and poor public school districts, and between public and private schools. The inspirational component of education flows largely from the quality of the adult/child mentoring relationship. Mentoring is a person-to-person dynamic; it is inherently labor intensive. The amount of money invested greatly affects the intensity of individual attention and instruction. Money can buy more teachers, more teachers' aides, more teacher training, more testing, more special education programs for the disabled, more psychological and academic counseling. Money can buy bright, clean, cheerful, inspiring classrooms, labs, playgrounds and sports facilities. Money can provide respectable salaries and benefits for teachers and administrators. Money can pay for bands, choirs, theater, arts, sports.

Schools alone, no matter how well funded, cannot wholly overcome the influences of disinterested or abusive parents, of delinquent peers, of drugs or crime, of an underculture that ignores or spurns education. But other things being equal, more money, wisely spent, will mean better education.

The truth is everywhere around us and is all but categorical: students from affluent, secure, supportive families who attend well-funded schools overwhelmingly flourish. In prosperous districts, the high school dropout rates are uniformly below 5 percent; the national average is around 20 percent; in the poorest districts, as mentioned, the rate hovers near 50 percent.

When reviewing the literature on equal opportunity and equal education one reads again and again the call to provide a good "basic" or "core" education for all of our children. Good? Basic? Core? What cowardly standards. What a statement about the value of our children. Why not every school an excellent school? Why should not every school offer a generous variety of artistic exposure and participative opportunities? Education, and the broad and balanced development of our children, should be the first and highest priorities of public investment. We can't afford it? Nonsense. The money needed to pay for better and equal education now resides in the mansions and summer houses and New York and Paris and Monte Carlo townhouses; and ski condos and yachts and Rolexes and Gucci's and fleets of motorcars of the super rich.

This point was made before, but it must be said again: our choice is either to invest up front in our children or to pay later for their problems and the problems they create for the rest of us. We either invest in good parenting, good schools, good communities, good jobs and good wages, or we pay later for police, prosecutors, prisons, drug and alcohol abuse, welfare, mental health problems and on and on. The quality of life difference—the quality of nation difference—between investing up front to create conscientious and productive citizens, or paying for, and living with, and mopping up after, the spill of poverty is enormous. If one is not moved by the ethics of the matter, one should at least be concerned about the macroeconomic efficiencies.

Equal opportunity, like equal protection under law, is another victim of poverty and inequality. Equal Opportunity for All is part of the political rhetoric of both liberals and conservatives. Is Equal Opportunity for All a sacred principle of our nation or is it to remain merely an expedient campaign slogan?

7

Poverty and the Sacred Principles of Our Nation:

Equal Protection Under Law

Civil Law and Criminal Law

Civil Law

Equal Protection Under Law is another sacred principle made impossible by poverty and inequality. One justice for the rich and another for the poor has become an American and international axiom.

Even the middle class is largely priced out of the civil courtroom. The cost of litigation often cows citizens from the defense of their rights. In civil litigation, time favors wealthy individuals and prosperous businesses that have the financial resources to delay and appeal until the average citizen simply can no longer bear the cost.

Most poor people are not criminals; their legal needs are civil, not criminal. The need for civil legal assistance for the poor is immense. These needs can be desperate and immediate. Some women need restraining orders against abusive husbands or boyfriends (fully one-sixth of all legal services for the poor are for domestic violence cases); some wives and husbands need to finalize long-needed divorces; some children need court orders to permanently remove them from abusive homes and move them toward adoption; other children languish in unresolved custody battles; some mothers need child support forcibly collected by the courts. Immigrants may need help procuring green cards so they can work; workers may need legal action against discrimination or against a firing they believe to be unjust. Or the legal issue may be a family's access to health care.

Such legal matters are of profound importance to the security of families. We can surely agree that these family legal issues need a timely response. This begs two questions: first, what can we do to reduce the internal turmoil and breakdown of families? Second, who should pay family-issue legal expenses? Should they be paid through government-funded legal service programs, or should we adjust the rules of the economic game so that every adult worker—and especially every parent—makes enough money to pay for, among other things, common family legal matters? I argue that both questions share the same answer. Families need and deserve to earn enough money, through work at good wages, to meet their full cost of living—this would include common, family legal expenses. Work at good wages, as opposed to tax dollars or charity dollars, should also provide enough comfort and security that the inherent pressures of childrearing are moderated.

The state of Ohio commissioned a study by The Spangenburg Group to identify the legal assistance needs for the poor in that state. Ohio's 590,000 low-income households (households at 125 percent of the poverty line) had approximately one million legal issues requiring attorney services. The states of Florida and Washington found a similar per household level of need. Projecting these values onto the nation, the nation's poor face about 24.8 million issues requiring legal counsel each year. An American Bar Association survey—suspect, of course, for its self-interest—estimates that each low-income household, on average, has 2.3 legal issues per year. This survey suggests that our nation's poor face perhaps 30 million legal issues each year.

Of these 30 million civil cases, the federal Legal Services Corporation handles about 1.7 million. State programs handle about one million more. Non-profits, pro bono legal work, law school aid programs, non-lawyer practitioners, and "alternative dispute resolution" agents handle a few million more. All together it is far from enough.

The Spangenburg Group and the Legal Service Corporation and the American Bar Association estimate that between 60 and 83 percent (depending on the survey referenced) of low income civil legal needs are unmet.

Resolving these civil legal issues, so many of which go to the heart of family stability and the protection of children, must be, I think, a priority for conservatives and liberals alike.

Equal Protection Under Law: Criminal Law

A case lost in civil court—even a case *won* in civil court—can mean financial disaster. The consequences of losing in a *criminal* proceeding can be catastrophic. It can mean loss of freedom, loss of a family's only income, loss of personal and professional reputation, loss of voting rights for life, and lifelong loss employment opportunities. Losing a criminal case often means divorce, estrangement from children and bankruptcy.

The terrors of such severe consequences provoked our Supreme Court to establish access to criminal defense counsel as a constitutional right. The United Nations stipulates access to counsel as a human right. Few rights are as essential or precious. Without competent, energetic counsel, the innocent, in the worst cases, can be executed. In 2002, Ohio's governor, a Republican, deemed it necessary to vacate all death sentences in that state because so many wrongful convictions were discovered—and these in capital punishment cases, the cases that receive the most scrutiny.

Inadequate, incompetent, uncaring defense for the indigent has become the shameful centerpiece of American criminal jurisprudence. Nationally, over 80 percent of criminal defendants are indigent. In the nation's largest seventy-five jurisdictions, almost 90 percent of defendants are indigent and require a public defender.

Poverty taints every aspect of the administration of justice, but none more than the right of good counsel. The huge caseloads of some public defenders make adequate consultation with clients and in-depth investigation of cases utterly impossible. The hourly rate paid to public defenders is one-third to one-tenth that of private rates, resulting in a marked lack of enthusiasm for indigent cases among attorneys. Attorneys who are forcibly appointed by judges to do public defense work have every incentive to dispose of cases quickly so they can get back to paying clients. The lawyer's apathy or sloppiness or laziness or hostility towards the client and the system are more the rule than the exception.

Nor does an attorney working at an inferior hourly rate of pay want any part of trials by jury. Decisions by judges are much quicker. Trial by jury means that the public defender must endure jury selection, deposing and preparing witnesses, and preparing articulate courtroom arguments. Every hour spent as a public defender deprives an attorney of better-paying cases. Plea bargaining is the instrument of choice for the quick disposal of cases.

In some jurisdictions judges shunt indigent cases to those attorneys who have proven themselves effective at extracting plea bargains from the accused. A lawyer's reputation for extracting quick pleas from defendants can get an attorney the inside track for state and county legal work (at a lower rate, but with regularity). Often "preferred" lawyers are retained under an annual and exclusive contract with the state or county. Judges much prefer a plea. They do not get bogged down in lengthy trials; dockets are cleared in time for golf in the afternoon. Quick pleas keep court operations within budget and keep the court's efficiency statistics (the number of cases processed per year) looking good—both of which benefit elected judges. In many jurisdictions, the police and judges and prosecutors view lawyers who try to stand up for their clients as troublemakers, attracting the wrath of judges and prosecutors in other cases.

A determined attorney can put irresistible pressure on indigent clients to plea-bargain. The indigent client knows that the court-assigned public defender is his only hope. The public defender can threaten a client with the maximum sentence of, say, five years if the case goes to trial, and then offer them six months to a year for a plea. Few poor defendants dare take the risk, regardless of innocence.

To wealth accrues all the advantages. Money makes it possible to hire the most reputable and aggressive lawyers. The rich can hire private investigators and expert consultants to scrutinize police evidence, to discover new evidence and to gather dirt to impugn witnesses. The wealthy can seldom be intimidated into a plea; a jury can always be demanded if deemed to their advantage. Sympathetic and expert witnesses can be tracked down, interviewed, coached on their testimony and then paraded before the jury. Enterprising defense teams can proffer endless objections and motions to break the rhythm and continuity of the prosecutor's case. Elaborate counter-theories, and real or red herring suspects, can be developed to confound jurors or create doubt.

The energetic defense counsel that money buys makes it possible for the affluent to stand up for their innocence (or to make the best of their guilt). The poor have the right on paper, but little right in practice.

There is a particularly painful irony in all this. The police, the prosecutors, the defense attorneys and the corrections administrators desperately want their professional integrity and want to do right—excepting of course the inevitable arsehole here and there. These public servants generally want to bring their personal pride and their professional service to the high ideals of justice. But income and wealth inequality taints the ideals of justice and their good efforts.

We must decide what principles and practices under our law (and under our various gods) we shall regard as universal and immutable. We must decide in practical, functional terms what Justice for All means, and how best to pay for it. We must decide if Equal Protection Under Law is a sacred principle of our nation or just a turn of phrase that draws snorts of cynicism.

8

Poverty and the Sacred Principles of Our Nation:

Representative Democracy

What ideals of human rights or nationhood would you defend with your death, or with the deaths of your children? How about representative democracy?

Representative democracy is an ideal on rank with freedom. It is perhaps freedom's guarantor. It is the centerpiece of our social contract. It is the basis upon which obedience to law and allegiance to nation can be rightly asked and demanded.

Equal voice is a common phrase, but not quite accurate. In a representative democracy, the majority, by numbers and by right, speaks with more volume and power. But legitimate democracy is not run by shear volume or raw power; legitimate democracy requires robust protection of the few and the quiet. A legitimate, representative democracy confers rights of access, protection, and effective redress of grievances to every citizen.

Under representative democracy, the majority can be a particular threat; the single voice and the minority voice require special amplification to be heard amid the many and the strong. We know this certainly when that singular voice is our voice.

The United States is a representative democracy only by the thinnest definition. Our Congress and legislatures, our state and national executives, our judiciary: none of them reflect the racial or gender or economic demographics of our nation.

Yes, we have universal suffrage; yes, we are more democratic than many other nations; and, yes, we can think, write or say what we please. But all of this is not sufficient. Effective public policy influence requires a sustained presence in the public eye and ear. Individuals and groups have effective influence only to the extent that they can print or broadcast their thoughts broadly and over time. This requires either the purchase of media time or the co-option or acquiescence of the media. Access to the media—sustained access—is granted almost exclusively to rare charisma or genius or celebrity—or to money.

A strained coalition of elites—the educated, the politically powerful and the economically powerful (with tremendous overlap among them)—commands almost total control of the U.S. mass media. The mass media's dependence on corporate advertising assures the media's compliance with a comfortable and common view. The public commentator who speaks outside the comfort zone of the advertisers or media executives will not be asked to speak again. On these terms, wealthy interests frame the public debate and national agenda. They do not do so comprehensively, of course; but in terms of sustained, mass coverage, their dominance is near-ubiquitous.

This coalition of academic and political and economic elites is often at odds. But they are bound together by their want of the power and privilege and prestige, manifest in knowledge and authority and money. The *economic* mission of this coalition, put simply, is to protect their professional advantage of power, income and wealth.

Egalitarian economic reforms occur almost exclusively when the abuses perpetrated by one of the elites so enrages the public that the politicians must act or fear for their office. Sometimes reforms occur when egalitarian interests incidentally coincide with those of the elites. Reforms also occur when the effects of the policy in question, or the behavior in question, become so apparent and so appalling that we are faced with a national crisis or international humiliation.

Money is the first determinant in getting and holding public power. A populist candidate can grasp political power momentarily, but without money he or she will not hold it for long. The financially weak are instantly targeted for removal by the opposing party. As the need for money to get elected increases, political candidates and parties find they must cater to wealth for the campaign contributions needed to survive politically.

A coalition of the lower middle class, the poor and the combined minorities, if unified and activated, would have overwhelming electoral power. Why does such a coalition not form or succeed?

The answer is complicated. Some of the poor are too preoccupied with personal or family survival to participate in politics. Others are too angry or too depressed to participate. Others believe that their vote means nothing. Others are not inclined to legitimize by their vote a system they believe oppresses them. Some are not by their temperament drawn to politics. And last, fatalism and apathy has a grip on many of the chronically poor.

Political participation rates among the poor have always been low. According to a 1997 study by Verba, Lehman-Schlozman, and Brady, persons in the lowest-income quintile volunteer approximately half as much time to political campaigns, are only three-fifths as likely to vote and contribute but one-fourteenth as much money to candidates and parties as does the top income quintile.

Furthermore, the underculture—the group that most desperately needs a political voice—is substantially incapacitated by its preoccupation with survival or depression or anger or general dysfunction.

Nor is political *candidacy* an option for the poor. Even the middle class is largely locked out of state and national office but for the rare exceptions of extraordinary personality or circumstance. Potentially successful candidates must possess wealth of such a magnitude that they can risk, and lose outright, thousands, if not millions, of dollars without jeopardizing the financial security of their families. Yet almost every politician has concocted some sort of born-in-a-log-cabin story.

Successful candidacy also requires large amounts of free time and flexible time. Running for office requires many free evenings and weekends. It requires much travel, even if only within a city. An eight-to-five, by-the-clock worker simply cannot break free to campaign. After work comes the commute and supper and family and fatigue. A legitimate, representative democracy simply must accommodate participation by working people beyond their access to a voting booth. Working people need a fair chance to hold office, most necessarily at the national level.

A successful candidacy, with rare exception, requires incumbency or party support or lots of personal money, and usually all three. The national rate of reelection of incumbents runs between 94 to 98 percent. The *primary* election is checkmate for non-affluent candidates. Voters seldom contribute enough money to a new candidate during the primary election to make him or her competitive. If a candidate is not seen as viable in the primary (usually *because* they do not have sufficient personal wealth to finance their own campaign), the party will not step forward with financial assistance until the unlikely event that the candidate reaches the general election. For the poor, and most of the middle class, the door to political office is closed.

It is a common belief that those who gain power deserve that power. This is the happy pretension of those in power. Whereas it almost certainly is true that there is a higher incidence of clinical learning impairment and ignorance within the lower economic classes, there are still plenty of smart, well-educated, insightful, leadership-worthy individuals among the poor and middle class who could admirably serve as legislators and executives.

The wealthy candidates who do win office are indeed rigorously tested by political campaigns for their perseverance and powers of articulation and fundraising. But the winners are almost always egocentric, aggressive, power-accruing personalities. These qualities have their uses, but they are not at the center of good human character. It is not unreasonable to think that perhaps persons of more modest financial means, more common experience, and more modesty generally, might better represent and serve our nation.

The poor—and the middle class—warrant much higher numerical representation in our government. The poor deserve, perhaps have a right to, the financial resources to contribute to campaigns and to participate as candidates with some chance of success. Legitimate, representative democracy requires a proximate demographic and economic cross section of the nation's citizenry.

Are we to revere and defend representative democracy or mock it? Are we to allow poverty to exclude millions from political access and leadership? By what principle of democracy or ethics should the rich be permitted to buy public office and public power?

9

Poverty and Big Government

Anyone who hates big government should hate poverty. Huge numbers of poor people require huge bureaucracies to deal with their problems. Not only must government deal with the problems of the poor, we also demand that government deal with the problems that the underculture creates for the rest of us.

Government is forced to act. When poverty ends in violent crime and drug trafficking and child abuse, every social class, rich and poor, demands action. Politicians clamor to respond with more social programs or more prisons.

Government is now under more pressure than ever to respond to societal dysfunction. The job instability and low wages that once distressed only the bottom 20 percent of workers now affect the lower echelons of the middle class, and the middle class cannot be ignored politically. The result is thin, but bipartisan, support for an interminable list of transfer programs, some absolutely necessary, some needless, some effective, some ineffectual, but all subject to the inefficiencies inherent in large bureaucracies.

Government is also forced to act because of the heinousness of some of the behaviors and consequences associated with poverty. Legislators of all ideologies cringe in horror at stories about the homeless freezing to death on the streets, the elderly freezing to death in their homes, children being beaten and tortured, teens being shot randomly. Such events become an embarrassment to the body politic and to the administrations in power. Politicians cannot forever avert their eyes or twiddle thumbs.

The demand upon government to protect the children is particularly loud. Conservatives and liberals alike hear the call. Even the most callous politician can sense the pragmatic consequences of writing off the millions of children in the underculture. Some politicians would like to limit welfare only to programs that directly benefit children. But they cannot. Most politicians see that the fate of the children is linked to the financial and emotional stability of the parents. The parents must be helped, like them or not. It is that or make the children wards of the government.

Poverty produces endless and time-consuming public policy conundrums. The President and Congress, our governors, our state legislatures and city councils, all are eternally entangled in every imaginable (and unimaginable) problem with poverty at the center or at the edges. Whether it be civil rights issues or voter registration or police profiling or access to education, government must deal with the consequences of poverty and inequality. Even petty matters like parking ticket fines and bus fares and public park use fees require politicians to determine how much money the poor can pay and which other income groups are going to subsidize the poor through taxes and fees. These disputes become ideological spats or outright rumbles between the political parties, grinding up vast amounts of executive and legislative time that could be better used. At every turn the hydra of poverty raises one of its heads.

To illustrate how governments are compelled into action, let us look at what happens when kids end up in poverty. First they must be fed, housed, clothed and given access to medical care. Children cannot manage for themselves; they must either be made wards of the state, or government assistance must be channeled through the parents or through surrogate parents. Government, in the worst cases, must pay for almost the entire market basket of family needs.

We demand that the father help support his family. But the father often cannot because chronic unemployment or low wages make it impossible for him to provide even for himself. Even worse, the underculture has socialized many young men to believe that it is morally acceptable to abandon their children. Government must act. Child protective service agents, or the police, must be employed to track down the delinquent fathers; prosecutors and social workers must petition the court to order child support; special family courts must be set up to hear the cases; elaborate bookkeeping and monitoring systems must be set up and administered to track the cases. More agents and police and social workers and judges are needed if the fathers subsequently refuse to pay. In some cases, space in the county jail must be found for them. We must pay for it all.

Not only must many children of the underculture be counseled and financially supplemented because of the neglect of the *absent* parent, so must they often be counseled and protected because of abuse by the *active* parent. Poor, single parents—especially teens—often feel imprisoned by parenthood. Most teens simply are not ready for such constraining and relentless responsibility. When the father is absent, both the human comradeship and the helping hand the mother needs are missing. Poverty plays a central role in this sense of entrapment. Poverty leaves little extra money for day trips or an evening out or a weekend getaway. Many of these trapped single parents become emotionally imbalanced or go seriously nuts. Research shows that parents who feel trapped by their children often abuse their children. The rate of child abuse is ten to twenty-two times as high for the poor as for the middle class. Government is again called upon. Programs such as respite day care and head start and summer programs are set up to get the child into a positive environment and to give single parents some time off. We pay for it all through government programs because unstable work and low wages make it impossible for poor parents to pay for the services themselves.

When abuse is confirmed, the children cannot be left in the home. Short-term protective foster care programs must be set up. Governments must also set up programs to attempt to rehabilitate the abusive parents. When this fails, vast amounts of investigative and prosecutorial and court time are required to revoke the custody rights of the biological parents so that adoption can proceed. While the legal process grinds on, the government must pay for long-term foster care. Government must also help search for and screen adoptive parents, either through the direct efforts of government agencies or through contracts with private adoption services.

And then there are the *disabled* children of poor families who cannot afford private health insurance or whose employers do not provide insurance. Federal and state governments are forced to create incredibly expensive programs—the mammoth Medicaid program being the centerpiece, with Supplemental Security Income and state-run children's insurance funds filling in the cracks.

Not only do severely and chronically poor families exhibit much higher rates of child abuse, but the spouses or partners also abuse one another. Spousal and intimate partner abuse in the underculture is epidemic. Again, we demand that government do something. Child Protective Service agents must take the children from the parents to a safe environment—usually foster care. Police must be given special training for these especially dangerous confrontations with the parents. Yet more social service agents and police must be hired. More court time and judges must be funded. Spousal abuse programs are set up to try to reform the abuser and to treat the victim. Battered women's shelters must be set up. County jails and state prisons must be enlarged to make room for the batterers. Probation and parole systems must be set up. Again, government has no choice but to respond. Again, we pay for it all.

Conservatives bristle and scream at having to pay for these social programs. We hate watching the kids get the worst of it. What to do? The moral imperative is upon us.

We—government—must act. There is no choice. Enough "compassionate conservatives" vote with the liberals to keep new programs coming and old ones running.

Government and the elderly poor also have an expensive relationship.

A 1997 study by the Center on Budget and Policy Priorities found that 47.6 percent of all elderly people had incomes below the poverty line before the receipt of Social Security. That figure for 2003 is 49 percent. Even *after* the receipt of Social Security payments, 11.9 percent of the elderly remained below the poverty line. In 2003 the median net worth of persons over sixty-five years of age was just over $100,000. That generally represents a small house, a piddling of depreciable assets in the form of old furniture and an old car, and perhaps $20,000 in financial assets. If this person put all $100,000 of their net worth in financial assets (which they cannot), they might generously glean $8,000 in annual income, an income below 50 percent of the poverty line. Remember, this is the median wealth; this describes half of the population over sixty-five.

Social Security became law because tens of millions of our citizens found it all-but-impossible to save. That is exactly the situation today. Social Security is a forced retirement savings plan. (It is, more precisely, a pay-as-you-go structure.) For most persons, their retirement "savings" are nothing more that FICA taxes, garnished from their paychecks.

And what about Medicare and Medicaid? Government has been forced into healthcare administration because about 45 million of us cannot afford health insurance or cannot get insurance through our employers. Medicare and Medicaid were established because the widespread and horrific health tragedies suffered by the elderly poor, and by the children of the poor, finally shamed government into action. It is Social Security that pulls half of our seniors just barely up to the poverty line, and it is Medicare that saves tens of millions of our seniors from bankruptcy and destitution. This is not the slightest exaggeration. My own parents, among the most frugal and hard working folks who ever walked the planet, were, in the end, saved by Medicare.

The elderly have many unique needs. Government has been pressed to provide emergency energy assistance (for heating and air conditioning), home insulation programs, furnace replacement programs, meals on wheels, in-home health care, adult daycare centers for the chronically impaired and much more. Supplemental Security Income helps the aged, blind and disabled, with heavy emphasis on the elderly.

I have fleetingly alluded to thirty or so federal means-tested programs; there are just over eighty-four of them. And I have not discussed a hundred other federal and state transfer programs whose purpose, in part, is to respond to the economic needs of the middle and lower classes.

Poverty forces government to act, bringing to bear government's inherent inefficiencies. Poverty, created by unstable employment and low wages and mal-distribution of our national income, throws us into one social crisis after another. One needy group after another presents itself. When a social problem becomes insufferable, politicians act, sometimes out of compassion, sometimes out of national humiliation, but usually out of fear of public outrage and losing their seat.

This nation acts, it seems, in every way except the way it should. We are forever chasing symptoms. The diseases are unstable work, low wages, and the unconscionable mal-distribution of our national income and wealth. In short, the problem is poverty. The problem is all the stress and dysfunction and antisocial behavior that follow. It is the poisonous culture of poverty.

As citizens, as a nation, we must come to see how poverty strips the cash out of our wallets and the quality out of our lives. We must come to see the grotesque systemic inefficiencies that poverty, crisis by crisis, puts upon us.

Business is able to get by with hiring labor at below the true cost of labor (below what it costs a worker to live) because government has entered into an implicit agreement with business: that government will make up the difference between what business pays its workers and what it actually costs a human being to live by maintaining a huge matrix of welfare and transfer programs. Business gets a cheap ride on the back of taxpayers and workers, who are one-and-the-same—you and I who work and pay taxes. Business gets cheaper labor; government picks up the resulting costs of poverty, in effect subsidizing businesses' cheap labor out of the public treasury. This is one form of what liberals like to call corporate welfare. All of the cost of the labor contained in a product should show up in the price of that product. Subsidizing businesses' labor costs with welfare and transfer programs creates false values in the marketplace: product prices that do not reflect the true value of labor in the products we buy.

This subsidization creates massive systemic inefficiencies because instead of having a prosperous citizenry making good wages and making its own best economic decisions with its own money, our government is forced to become caretaker and parent of the poor—police enforcer, judge and prosecutor and public defender, warden, drug addict rehabilitator, healthcare administrator, retirement fund administrator, and on and on. It is bad governance, bad business, and bad economics.

10

The Total Dollar-cost of Poverty in the United States

Putting a precise dollar-cost on poverty is not possible. But precision is not needed. What we need is a sense of the magnitude of the cost of poverty relative to overall economic output.

The total cost identified below understates the case, perhaps by as much as 30 percent. Many costs were omitted because they did not warrant detailed research. Some opportunity costs are included; some are not because data is not available. Opportunity costs, in this usage, are defined as the costs our society incurs because large amounts of labor must be employed to respond to poverty—extra social service workers, police, judges, prosecutors, etc.—preventing those individuals from doing other productive work. The cost of this misused labor is massive, easily approaching an additional one trillion dollars per year.

The Approximate Total Dollar-cost of Poverty, per year, in the United States (in billions in 2003 dollars)

The approximate cost *of that portion of all crime*
  that is estimated to be associated with poverty.
  (The total cost of *all* crime is estimated to

be between 1.2 to 1.3 trillion annually.
Please see this footnote for assumptions
and justifications)[1] $600.0 billion.

Welfare: all income-tested cash and
non-cashprograms[2]   570.0

Other transfer payment programs that exist
substantially to keep citizens out of poverty,
to respond to the needs of the poor, or to
extend access or opportunity to the poor[3]   711.0

Charity: defined as private social service
programs targeted to the poor (food
banks, homeless shelters, battered
women's shelters, youth shelters, the
social service component of United
Way, faith-based social programs,
part of the cost of privately funded
or subsidized drug and alcohol abuse
programs)[4]   53.0

Uncompensated care in public and private
hospitals: emergency and non-emergency
losses absorbed by the hospital and, in total
or in part, passed on to other insured or
self-paying patients through higher charges[5]   23.2

Private Security: guards, electronic surveillance,
alarms, fences, K-9 units, lighting, padlocks,
safes, vaults, weapons and equipment[6]   41.9

Federal, state, local child protective services,
provided through non-means-tested programs;
includes foster care, adoption services, family
preservation programs, child support
enforcement (net cost of), plus other misc.[7]   14.4
                                                                          _____

THE APPROXIMATE TOTAL COST
OF POVERTY IN THE U.S (2003 dollars) $ 2.014 trillion
per
year

Cost of Poverty per Capita per Year
(289.4 mil. Pop., 2003) $ 6,960.

Cost of Poverty per Employed Person
per Year (138.5 mil., 2003) $ 14,540.

Cost of Poverty in 2003 as a
Percent of 2003 GDP 17%

Subcategories of the Cost of Poverty (in billions, 2003 dollars)

[The costs listed below *are not in addition to* the costs listed above. These costs are *within* the above costs. These subcategories are separated to highlight the major areas of cost and to highlight certain hidden costs of poverty. The values below include many overlapping costs between these subcategories. *These subcategory values should not be summed together.* For example, the cost of violent crime, child abuse and spousal abuse contain large medical cost components. These medical costs are also contained in the crime-related medical costs subcategory. The values below *do not* represent *total* U.S. expenditures within each category; *they represent only that portion of total U.S. expenditures estimated to be related to poverty.*]

Crime related subcategories of cost

Violent Crime only (only that portion
    attributable to poverty)[8] $ 509.3

Medical costs for physically injured police,
    victims, bystanders and criminals[9]   60.1

Police, courts, prosecutors, parole boards,
    probation officers, jails, prisons,
    halfway houses, etc.[10]   118.8

Crime victim assistance programs[11]   95.0

Drug abuse (estimated poverty-associated
    portion only); use, distribution, the
    accost of crimes committed by addicts
    to buy drugs, addictions, treatment
    programs, education programs, HIV/AIDs
    from needle-transferred crack and heroin use,
    estimated lost productivity from premature
    deaths and mental impairment, family
    breakup (divorce, child protection, foster
    care, adoption resulting from child abuse cases)[12]   92.8

The criminal justice related costs of child abuse
    (does not include the medical and other
    social welfare costs of child abuse)[13]   72.5

Estimated cost of future/adult crime
    associated with child abuse[14]   50.3

Estimated lost future/adult productivity as a result
    of mental and physical impairments
    from child abuse[15]   23.0

The social services cost of child abuse[16]   22.5

Spousal abuse (criminal, social service and
other costs: loss of life, physical and mental
medical costs, battered women's shelters, work
hours lost because of medical recovery and
stalking, criminal justice costs)[17] 19.9

Insurance payouts for property destruction and
property replacement due to crime[18] 22.5

Providing public defenders for the indigent[19] 2.6

Itemization of Means-tested Cash and Non-cash Welfare and Transfer Program Expenditures: total federal, state, and local expenditures: (Estimated 2003 expenditures based on 2002 released data, adjusted for inflation to approximately reflect maintenance of service; all values are in billions):

Healthcare related programs $ 307.9 billion

Medicaid	281.4 billion
Medical care for low-income veterans	8.9
Children's health insurance	5.5
General health assistance	5.1
Indian health services	3.1
Maternal and infant care	1.4
(plus 3 other programs)	

Cash Assistance 11.4 billion

Supplemental Security Income	42.0 billion
EITC	30.3
TANF	14.3
Foster care	9.4
Child Tax Credit	5.5
General Cash Assistance	3.6
Adoption assistance	2.6
(plus 4 other programs)	

Food Assistance   42.0

     Food stamps   26.3 billion
     Subsidized school lunches   6.6
     Women, Infants, Children   4.8
     Child and adult care   1.7
     (plus 8 other programs)

Housing Benefits   38.8

     Sec. 8 low income housing   20.1 billion
     Low-rent public housing   8.8
     Elderly and disabled housing   1.0
     Rural rental assistance   .8
     (plus 13 other programs)

Education Benefits   33.2

     Pell grants   12.4 billion
     Head Start   8.8
     Subsidized Stafford Loans   8.2
     Federal work-study   1.1
     (plus 10 other programs)

Services   24.2

     Child care and development   9.4 billion
     TANF (services only)   6.6
     Title XX block grants   2.9
     TANF (child care only)   2.6
     Homeless assistance   1.1
     (plus 4 other programs)

Jobs and training		8.5

TANF (work only)	2.9 billion
Job Corps	1.6
Other youth programs	1.1
Adult activities	1.0
(plus 7 other programs)	

Energy Aid		2.4

Low-income energy assistance	2.0 billion
Weatherization	.4

**Total Federal, State and Local Cash
    and Non-cash Means-tested
    Expenditures, 2003** (including
    non-listed programs; values are rounded.)   **$ 570 billion**

I want to leave you with three points:

First: poverty has its claws in our wallets every second of every hour of every day. The notion that cheap goods created by cheap labor are a boon to us all is a fool's illusion. We may pay less for goods produced by cheap labor, but we pay much more for the police, courts, prisons, drugs, child abuse and all the other costs of poverty summarized in the last eight chapters.

Second: most people think that we have paid the bill for poverty when we pay for welfare. Welfare is but a modest fraction of the total cost of poverty—somewhere between one-forth and one-fifth of the total cost of poverty.

Third: poverty creates massive systemic inefficiencies. Every dollar and every hour spent responding to avoidable poverty represents human labor that could be, and should be, applied to more productive pursuits. This misuse of labor represents lost productive opportunities, one of the "opportunity costs" of poverty.

11

Closing Remarks

If you still do not believe that poverty costs this nation (you and me as taxpayers) massive amounts of money every year; if you do not believe that these cumulative, year-upon-year expenditures represent massive systemic inefficiencies, or if you do not believe that poverty and inequality directly threaten yourself, your family, your income and your property; if you do not believe that poverty's insidious consequences poison our national quality of life as well as our personal souls; if you do not believe that poverty undermines and mocks the most sacred principles of our nation, the great ideals for which we flourish our flag and pledge our allegiance and send our sons and daughters to their deaths to defend; if you do not believe that much of terrorism and international war and civil revolution are linked to the world's abject, desperate, hopeless, starvation-poverty, as well as the taunting, envy-creating juxtaposition of wasteful, ostentatious lifestyles contrasted against great need and misery; then you are, not to put too fine a point on it, beyond all intellectual and moral help.

I am sick of the whole miserable business of poverty and I wish the same for you. Our daily news is a heartbreaking chronicle of the lashings-out of the American underculture, and of the interminable wars and acts of terrorism being waged all over our planet by people so economically marginalized or desperately impoverished or so embittered and vacant of hope, that life itself means little or nothing to them. For all of our anguish over September 11, 2001, that act of terrorism was but a small taste from the roiling cauldron of human malice and discontent that poverty and inequality create or exacerbate.

Our nation is awash in material wealth, but material wealth does not make a nation great. Our soup kitchens and food banks and homeless shelters and emergency rooms are lined up out the doors with the poor. There are veritable villages of homeless people beneath our cities' bridges and viaducts, filthy, sick, drunk— an estimated one-third of them mentally ill. Our battered women's and youth shelters are full, with extra mattresses lined up in the hallways. Two million of our citizens are in federal and state prisons; over 500,000 more are in county jails. Forty-five million citizens are without health insurance. We discover as parents that our primary mission is to protect our children from the culture we have created.

Poverty is at the center of most of these problems, and at the edges of many more. Severe or sustained or chronic poverty creates stress, depression, anger, hopelessness, apathy. It frustrates courtship and marriage. It increases the incidence of divorce. It creates unspeakable anxiety in the hearts of parents about the well-being of their children.   Severe or sustained or chronic poverty often ends in emotional imbalance and mental illness. Poverty leads to antisocial, criminal, and sociopathic values and behaviors. It leads to coarseness and incivility and meanness in interpersonal relations. It leads to irrationality, and individual and family dysfunction.

Severe or sustained or chronic poverty undermines self-respect and leads to self-abuse and abuse of others. It leads to selfishness and a preference for easy and immediate gratification. It crushes thoughtful plans and hopeful dreams. It undermines health and significantly reduces average life expectancy. Poverty creates its own self-reinforcing, self-perpetuating culture. It degrades and corrupts. It poisons reason, conscience, soul, society, and the body politic.

The dollar-cost is horrific and the spiritual cost is incalculable. The murders, the rapes, the assaults, the child abuse, the spousal abuse; the subtle, generalized fear; the distrust; the loss of respect for government and law. All of it haunts the conscience of anyone who thinks and cares.

Many thoughtful conservatives believe that if the members of the underculture would act more responsibly—that is, obey the law, control their sexual propensities, and answer to their parental duties—our nation's problems would be significantly reduced. Many of these conservatives assert that the problem is not poverty, but moral and ethical deficiency. There most surely is a breakdown of morality and ethics in the underculture, but what causes this breakdown?

The greater truth is that severe or sustained or chronic poverty almost always precedes criminal behavior, as well as a wide variety of antisocial behaviors. Poverty is almost always part of the history of the sociopath. Our prisons are filled with the poor. The underculture, where values and behaviors are most corrupted, is, almost to a person, composed of individuals who have endured severe or sustained poverty.

Our nation, our political leadership, and each of us, are ethically answerable for this poverty. We who would be conservatives must answer to a test of the sincerity of our stated principles.

My conservative friends are quick to point to the corruption of family values. We demand personal moral responsibility. You have probably read about Maslow's hierarchy of needs. Maslow's finding is that persons generally do not, and cannot, turn their attention to higher ethical issues and self-actualization until their basic physical and psychological needs are met. Individuals have great difficulty functioning at higher intellectual levels when preoccupied with a struggle for bare existence or when fighting with their lower emotions. Severe or sustained or chronic poverty forces one's attention onto self-preservation, selfishness, and grasping for available gratifications. This is not the response of all persons; this is not the response of most poor persons; but this is the response of many persons in the poverty culture and in the underculture. The moral rectitude and the functional good sense we demand of persons living with the stresses of poverty, and living within the poverty culture, are often simply beyond the powers of the average Joe or Jane.

Conservatives are rightly proud of holding up moral ideals. But to sustain an economic system that permits so few to have so much while so many have so little is an affront to the most fundamental human and spiritual values. Such severe maldistribution of our national prosperity cannot be justified by any humanistic philosophy or before any god.

We demand family financial responsibility. But financial responsibility is a *functional* competency. Functional competencies are learned. They require awareness and skills and habits. Political responsibility requires self-education and the cultivation of public interest; it requires listening skills and empathy; it requires forming a commitment to, and a habit of, voting. Work responsibility requires the development of communication and teamwork skills; it means learning how to set goals, sensitizing oneself to matters of urgency, efficiency and safety; it means learning appropriate dress and speech; it means getting to work on time. Personal and family financial responsibility requires skills in budgeting, and staying within a budget; it means prioritizing expenditures and developing the discipline to stick to those priorities; it means developing plans for saving and investing.

Such skills are learned by doing—and not learned by not doing. If a person can barely muster together pocket money, financial planning becomes little more than emptying one's wallet for necessities, then spending the last ten bucks on pizza and beer. The skills and habits of family money management are learned, in part, by having money to manage.

Conservatives demand personal empowerment rather than government empowerment. Nothing confers power and opportunity like money, and nothing truncates power and opportunity like poverty. Money in many ways is freedom. Money is opportunity in many forms. Money is access and voice. And when the rules of the economic game result in tens of millions of our citizens being unable to take care of themselves financially, where does power default to? In large part, it defaults to precisely where we prefer it not go, to government: as engineer and administrator and monitor and enforcer of public assistance, as warden for the criminals, as protector of abused children and spouses, as parent to abandoned children, as healthcare insurer and healthcare provider. All of it together costs us trillions every year, year upon year. When conservatives demand personal empowerment, is the demand made on behalf of all citizens, or is it made for the advantage of the rich and their families? Is the conservative demand for individual empowerment an earnest appeal in behalf of all citizens, or is it a demand intended to pander to a rich political constituency? The earnestness of our statements about broad personal empowerment is rightly questioned.

We pride ourselves on our pragmatism and prudence. Poverty undermines both. The macroeconomic losses—at least two trillion annually, excluding, it is estimated, another trillion in opportunity-costs—should bristle the neck hairs of every conservative and every businessperson. The economic and spiritual cost to our nation of having so many of the children of the underculture lost to drugs and imprisonment is unnecessary and unconscionable.

Poverty is bad for business. When workers are denied sufficient income, they are, as consumers, denied purchasing power. Tens of millions of our citizens cannot buy beyond their basic needs, and many of those purchases are made with public assistance dollars. Poor people buy less of everything that business makes. Good incomes create product demand and jobs, just as jobs create income and demand.

> [My conservative colleagues are quick to remind me that if wages go up, prices must go up also. This suggests inflation, without real gains—a serious dilemma that must be answered. This will be discussed in some detail in "Appendix One: Some Modest Proposals." For the moment, permit me to say only that there are substantial offsetting savings for consumers, savings that will in the long run more than offset price increases. Please see Appendix One.]

There is little pragmatism or prudence in the current rules of the economic game, not regarding raw systemic efficiency nor national stability nor good social or business sense nor spiritual wisdom. The juxtaposition between what our nation is now, with its current levels of poverty and inequality, and what it might be with poverty greatly reduced, is veritably black to white.

Conservatives need to temper their worship of freewheeling free enterprise. Freedom is the siren song of conservatism, and a siren to us all. We all want to do as we please. Even disciplined conservatives must occasionally be "tied to the mast" to keep them from the temptations that pleasure seeking and fortune seeking draw out of human nature. Our desire to do as we please is particularly strong in matters of money making.

But we can no longer do just as we please economically. The power of modern humanity—the mechanical brute force of our machines, our technical finesse, our organizational sophistication, the instantaneous global reach of information and capital—has exponentially accelerated the rate of cultural and institutional change. Genetic engineering, cloning, nuclear tinkering, the creation of synthetic molecules—all of it is being pressed forward pell-mell, most of the research being done in proprietary secrecy, with public safety in a tug of war against the pursuit of profit. Added to it all is the dark likelihood that nuclear or biological or chemical technology will filter through black markets into the hands of terrorists. Cataclysmic possibilities suggest themselves. The percentage of carbon dioxide in the atmosphere is increasing rapidly; the ozone hole in our atmosphere is admitting unprecedented levels of ultraviolet radiation to the earth's surface; several species have exhibited sudden and inexplicable mutations. What does all this mean? Are we seeing smoke or apocalyptic fire? No one knows.

The uncertainly and the severity of the potential consequences beg for a broader definition of conservatism. Not the conservatism of unbridled free marketeering, but rather the conservatism of caution, wisdom and active management. A conservatism that focuses upon long-term, systemic sustainability, and upon the health and welfare and prosperity of all people.

Governments, once seen as consumer protectorates, have proven no match for quick and nimble corporations. If one nation says no, another says yes or says nothing. Businesses flee across borders from water and air pollution controls, flee from toxic disposal regulations, flee from organized labor, flee from worker safety regulations, flee from the minimum wage, flee from taxes.

Louder than the perplexed and alarmed cries of progressive politicians and concerned scientists is the wail from all quarters for jobs, jobs, jobs. Conservative and centrist politicians have in effect said to corporate America, "Do as you will but create more jobs." In response, corporate America is importing, outsourcing and moving factories overseas as fast as they can figure out how to do so.

Public power (representative government) simply must have supremacy over corporate power. This is especially true in areas such as the market for human beings (the labor market), the transfer of jobs to other nations, and trade content and balances. Collective society, as manifest in our governments, has lost control of the speed and direction of economic development. With precious few exceptions, business and labor are being carried off by runaway multinational corporatism with power so colossal that governments wither before it.

I also appeal to my conservative colleagues to look at free markets more realistically. Free markets do many things marvelously, magically well. Free markets, however, do some things very poorly or not at all. Free markets do a superb job of drawing out innovation and pushing down prices. The value of the inventiveness and efficiencies fostered by free markets is almost impossible to overstate. But the many ethical and functional conundrums created by free markets require occasional human intervention.

If the only concern of an economy was setting the price of, say, steel, or determining who gets the next set of golf clubs, all might be well. But free markets do not just traffic in ingots of steel and golf clubs, they also distribute human necessities. The terms of trade are: if you have the money you may have the product or service; if you do not have the money, you may not. It matters not one whit whether a person has a set of golf clubs, but it matters gravely if a family cannot buy food or housing or heating oil or the health care it needs.

And most troublesome, we have permitted free markets—the labor market— to determine the dollar value of human beings. The value of a human being on this market ranges from less than zero (no one will hire them, and they must live on money taken from other workers) to tens of millions a year for one person's salary and benefits.

The sociological problems and system inefficiencies begin when the labor market says to too many people, "You are not needed" or, when the labor market says, "I will hire you if you are willing to work for whatever I am willing to pay, regardless of how much it costs you to live." The trouble continues when the market says, "Bob, Sally: you and your children are worth little or nothing; George, Margaret: here are millions to live in excess and ostentation and to give your children advantages that other parents can only dream of."

If ingots of steel sit idle, they sit without need or complaint. If a set of golf clubs is sold for half its true value, the clubs care not at all. If human beings are forced into idleness, or are paid less than it costs them to live securely, those affected care desperately. Horrendous psychological pressures immediately bear down on them. A human beings has ceaseless and immediate and substantial fiscal needs that must be met regardless of the individual's productivity, intellect, judgment, inventiveness or energy. If the needs and reasonable wants and spiritual aspirations of human beings are not given some measure of fruition, the angriest of them may first steal the wheels off your car, may next stick a gun in your ribs for your wallet, may next shoot you or rape your daughter for the mere fun of it, and may finally burn down large parts of your city.

To a substantial degree, personal income must be protected, in part for the worker/consumer/citizen's sake, *but primarily to safeguard the positive development of the next generation.* Some people, when they lose their income, are agile and quickly back on their feet; others are tough and grit through to the next job with only minor mental bruises. But few people can survive severe or sustained or chronic poverty with their heads still screwed on straight. They may not become criminals or go nuts and become sociopaths, but they may become imbalanced or quirky or lose their confidence. And a few do go nuts, just as surely as might you or I. It is from this troubled population—now including a new population of about twelve million working poor—that the underculture arises.

The labor market—the market in human beings—trades in a sentient and fragile commodity. Some economic efficiency, some of the speed of the economic churn, needs to be moderated to accommodate the need of the average human animal for security and stability.

Globalization has created the most ominous labor market dynamic. Trade and multinational corporatism have placed American workers in head-to-head competition for jobs and wages with ultra-low-priced foreign labor. American businesses and workers are losing sales and jobs at an unprecedented rate. During economic expansions, we are creating far fewer jobs than we otherwise would. There is no end to the supply of cheap foreign labor and almost no end to the list of nations that desperately want corporate investment and will let corporations do as they please. For Americans, trade makes many products cheaper, but inflation-adjusted wage rates for the lowest-paid workers have gone down even more than product prices. American business and American labor must protect themselves from these severe cross-border imbalances in labor cost and competitive advantage.

My conservative colleagues insist that markets are best left alone. That is broadly true, but not as true as many conservatives would wish. Markets primarily serve efficiency. Permit me to say again, that efficiency is not the sole object of a legitimate economic system; the betterment of the condition each individual participant in that economic system, and the betterment of the collective society are the larger objectives. We need to see clearly what markets do well and what markets do not do well. This same caution applies to the international trade markets, the flow of and labor-value and production and capital across borders. Free markets are not what they are cracked up to be by far-right conservatives. A wiser, more prudent conservatism needs to prevail.

I would also ask my conservative colleagues to revisit the notion of investment in a social context. Business investment is like public investment in this simple sense: if there is no investment, there is no return on investment. Our nation has fundamentally two overarching resource allocation options: either we invest up-front in schools, libraries, sports, theater, music, sex and family education, boy's and girl's clubs; or we pay later for ignorance, violence, broken families, police, prisons, drugs, and much more. By investing wisely up-front, not only do we save money and gain efficiency in the long run, but, consider, I beg you, the difference in the quality of our lives between these two allocation approaches.

If things are so bad, why don't things change? It is a vital question.

For the average citizen, a robust debate about inequality on, say, public TV (the networks won't touch the topic) will incite violent snoring. Middle America is not yet roused by appeals for economic justice. Middle America works hard and, by definition, makes enough to get along. They do not readily understand why everyone cannot do the same. Poverty, inequality, discrimination, marginal-ization, have no compelling meaning for the middle class or the rich. The middle class clings to stability, fearful that change may threaten their position. The poor oscillate between rage and apathy and frustrated activism. The wealthy regard the system as approximately just, the system needing, if anything, adjustments in their favor. The poor, in the typical view of the well-off, get approximately what they deserve.

Our state and national politicians are, almost to the last person, rich. They see economic policy through the same lens of affluence and advantage as other rich individuals. Politicians are, in part, in comfortable agreement with the affluent social and professional company they keep; in part, brainwashed and greased with money by well-heeled lobbyists; in part, captives of wealthy campaign con-tributors; and, in part, captives of the pressures of the political crises of the moment. These pressures make thoughtfulness nearly impossible, and their des-perate dependence on large campaign contributions makes statesmanship nearly impossible. This, to a gastronomically upsetting degree, leaves the stewardship of our nation at the mercy of partisan strategists and effective fundraisers. In the end, most politicians, Republican and Democrat, see the greater service to their own reelection, and to their personal financial interests, to be through serving the wealthy. The poor, whose numbers could turn any election, do not make them-selves felt at the polls, nor can they buy access.

There is, in my view, no greater need in this nation than to establish a genuinely representative democracy. The absence of true representative democracy in the

United States is The Reason that the current extremes of maldistribution of income and wealth persist. No one should doubt that if the voices of low-income individuals were heard, and if it were possible (financially and emotionally and practically) for them to participate in the leadership of this nation in proportion to their numbers, our economic arrangements would be markedly different.

History does not bode well for income and wealth redistribution. History shows that the rich will fight for every last dollar. At this turn in time, the wealthy hold near-unprecedented percentage shares of income and wealth, and they want still more. When income and wealth redistribution start to bite into the lifestyle, power, influence, and prestige of the super rich they will politically hiss and scratch like cornered cats. In the end, only a true representative democracy will be able to effect and sustain any policy that seeks to redistribute income or wealth.

When politicians are elected who see it as their duty to serve all of our citizens, it is a curious possibility that income and wealth redistribution may represent a Magnificent Convergence of conservative and liberal principles. Conservatives, in part, want less government and greater personal responsibility. Liberals, in part, want a more equitable distribution of income and wealth. I am arguing that more personal responsibility will come with more income and wealth.

Liberals have had to swallow the bitter pill of failure regarding the dependency and temptations for abuse wrought by the worst of our welfare programs. Liberals have had to chasten their tendency to change corporate behavior by imposing costly regulations. Liberals, better appreciating the organic and tenacious nature of bureaucracies, now think two or three times before creating another one. Conservatives, I believe, now need to swallow some truth about the social and economic and moral costs of poverty and inequality.

Conservatives and liberals should seek together, in an earnest competition of ideas, the best answer to this question: on what practical and ethical terms should our national income and wealth be divided among us?

Our economic system is not an act of god or nature or fate. However difficult to fathom, it is not mystic. The rules of our economic game—our tax law, contract law, tort law, banking law, inheritance law, labor law, securities and exchange law, occupational health and safety law, environmental protection law, and more—are human contrivances from top to bottom. We have formed this system by our action and by our default. We can change it if we choose. We are responsible.

Appendix One

Some Modest Proposals

—About My Proposals

—Principles to Guide Policy

—Some Modest Proposals

-A New Type of Minimum Wage

-Trade and Globalization

-Recession Avoidance and Management

-Other Program Components

Appendix One

About My Proposals

But what to do? A small army of self-proclaimed visionaries and social engineers stand ready to counsel their schemes to anyone who will listen. Some of these visionaries are thoughtful academics, some are utopian-idealists, some geniuses, some crazies. Some are geniuses who also happen to be crazy. The visionaries who dare to act on their imaginings create a conundrum for governance: they are, at once, humanity's best hope and worst nightmare. Visionaries can be downright dangerous. Every decade or so, fate or human folly empowers a Napoleon or Hitler or Stalin or Rhodes or Mao or Pol Pot to remind us of what happens when people who believe they know The Truth take the political helm and attempt to force their views on everyone else. We are safe from these people only through institutional checks and vigilance. Yet, we fail to listen to new and original thought at our own peril.

That said, few, probably none, of these ideas are my own. Yet I do feel obliged to stop the criticism and say something constructive.

Political economy remains an art form. There is no chance of getting everything right. There is no chance of making everyone happy. There is no policy that will transfer exactly equal costs and benefits upon all citizens. Every bold plan or policy, whether contrived by seers or fools, is immediately twisted and thinned and bleached beyond recognition by wary politicians and selfish interests.

Only masochists or blockheads willingly step into this arena. Here are my ideas.

Appendix One: (continued)

Principles to Guide Policy

The rules of our economic game must insure that all families can make enough income to provide for the educational and social development of their children, and to provide development opportunities that are roughly comparable to the opportunities enjoyed by other children in their culture. Failing to provide roughly equal developmental opportunities is a violation of the human rights of the children left behind. Fundamentally, all families must be able to meet their financial responsibilities, including their saving and retirement needs. Beyond meeting its needs, every family deserves to be able to purchase some of its reasonable wants and to fulfill some of its modest aspirations.

A legitimate economic system must distribute the national income and the national wealth with enough equity that every citizen, family, and child can flourish. I argue that this distribution is best effected through stable work at a full-cost-of-living wage, not through low wages augmented by welfare and transfer programs.

The intergenerational passage of the hurtful values and behaviors of the poverty culture must be stopped. The fate of our nation is to large extent the fate of our families and children. If we do not protect the development of each child *with some considerable equality relative to the developmental opportunities given all other children we* condemn future generations to suffer the Pandora's box of problems that arise from poverty and inequality.

Without substantial changes in income and wealth distribution, tens of millions of our children will continue to be raised by frustrated, angry, abusive parents; with millions of children and adults being socialized by violence, meanness, criminality, distrust, crushed hopes; with the grown-children-now-parents, in turn, abusing and neglecting their own children; with young men walking away from their parental responsibilities; with families torn apart by stress and depression; and with the explosive pressures within the underculture precariously contained by welfare appeasement, inane entertainments, and mass imprisonment.

Political and economic support of the family is essential. Our nation must aggressively act to insure the spiritual development and economic viability of the next generation. Positive, balanced child development is the absolute, comprehensive, responsibility of all adults, particularly of community leaders. People may be born stupid, but they are not born bad. There is no human riffraff except that created by adult failures in our homes and in our culture. Children who are loved, educated, socialized and mentored through kind, respectful human interaction will turn out well. Children raised badly—abused, neglected, lectured to, humiliated, under-educated, and exposed to every manner of mean, selfish, antisocial behavior—will, with great frequency, turn out bad. Each of us shares in the responsibility for creating our "bad" citizens despite our pugnacious denials. We are responsible for the school that did or did not get built; the teacher or counselor that did or did not get hired, the boy's and girl's club that did or did not get built, the theater club or chess club or model airplane club that did or did not get started.

While it is true that a family's affluence does not guarantee a good home for that family's kids (rich and middle-class parents can be rotten parents), raising the income of our lowest-paid workers will *guarantee statistically* that many more kids live in stable homes and experience positive developmental opportunities.

Young men and women—especially young men—must witness and experience enough economic prosperity that they do not fear the financial responsibilities of marriage and family. Young men who cannot meet their own financial needs are disinclined to shoulder the financial responsibilities of a family. As discussed in chapter 2, poverty can humiliate and emasculate and disempower young men. Such disempowerment gives rise to other hurtful, power-imposing, power-grasping behaviors such as child and spousal abuse, and reaching for quick and easy gratifications.

Independently-living adults need sufficient income whether they are smart or dumb, shrewd or simple, whether they are commercially aggressive or artistic or spiritual by nature. The rules of the economic game must respond to the fact that some people can produce a thousand or a million times what it costs for them to live while others cannot even produce what they consume.

(This does not mean that persons of marginal economic productivity should receive incomes equal to persons who are insightful, creative, energetic, entrepreneurial, prudent. Perfect equality, or even approximate equality, can be as counterproductive as great inequality. Perfect income equality would ignore differences in merit. Modest levels of inequality serve positive economic purposes. It is the extremes that cause the trouble.

Some redistribution of income and wealth is necessary if the lowest-income individuals and families are to have the income and wealth they need.

Let me say this bluntly: the owners, managers and technical elites cannot be permitted to continue to take the huge over-share of income and wealth that they now command. The rich now command so much of the national income and wealth that there simply is not enough left over, when divided up, to meet the needs of the bottom 40 percent of our population. The bottom 40 percent of wealthholders controls only 3/10 of 1 percent of our nation's total private wealth, to be divided among them. The bottom 40 percent of workers controls only 12.5 percent of our nation's total private income, to be divided among them. If our national personal income were equally divided among all working individuals, each person would receive about $68,000 per year, or $136,000 per couple. As things are now, the average income of the bottom 20 percent of households is about $10,000. The lowest income 40 percent of our population is now being propped up in some measure by over eighty means-tested public assistance programs—welfare, Social Security, Medicare, Medicaid and dozens of other transfer programs. A more equitable income and wealth distribution can be struck which will still leave the super rich very rich indeed.

My fundamental proposition is that we eliminate both the super rich and the super poor—roughly, the top 2 percent and the bottom 30 to 40 percent. I suggest a scheme of substantially increasing the minimum wage. This will put downward pressure on the highest salaries and *simultaneously and automatically*, remove millions from the poverty roster and from the means-tested program rosters. If people have work that pays the full cost of living, they will, by and large, not need such programs.

I do not doubt that better minds can think of better ways to get money into the hands of the poor. In an ingenuous sort of way, I do not care what redistributive mechanisms are used.

I suggest as well that the potential gains in efficiency and quality of life created by more equitable income and wealth distribution are so profound that significant experimentation should be risked to find better economic structures.

Redistribution is best done through universally-available work and good wages, rather than through welfare and transfer programs.

Private-sector work is preferred for many reasons. But, if we are forced to choose between no work and government work, government work is surely better. If we are forced to choose between government work and government welfare, let us choose government work.

Government work need not be make-work. There is much public work that genuinely, indeed, desperately, needs to be done, and that will yield a generous return on the public investment dollar.

Government work can be used to help stabilize families' incomes. Steady work sustains a national work ethic. Steady work permits, and to some extent forces, families to better manage their money, rather than live moment to moment. Steady work fosters middle-class tastes, values and behaviors. This runs the gamut from a well-kept lawn to dress to speech to physical posture to one's educational attainment expectations for one's children.

Again, I want to convince you that it is categorically better that redistribution be effected through work at good wages than through low-wage jobs supplemented by welfare and transfer programs.

Economic dynamism and efficiency, as well as international competitiveness, are essential.

The positive effects of materialism—material plenty—should not be underestimated. Material plenty is more than just the per capita production of golf clubs. Materialism includes safe, warm housing, clinics and hospitals, schools and universities, and a wide array of consumer goods that inspire and inform and protect. Our safety, comfort, and education—as well as our liberation from ceaseless toil made possible by modern appliances and tools and manufacturing processes—all facilitate empathy and ethics. It is freedom from material scarcity that frees our bodies and minds for higher purposes. It is efficiency that creates the economic surplus that allows us to build institutions of higher learning, libraries, symphonies, good highways and all our other things that give us the leisure and health and joy that are the rewards of our day-to-day work.

Most of us *want* our economic system to be fair, but we *need* it to work. "To work" means that the system must not merely *tend towards* maximizing micro and macroeconomic efficiency, but that our economy must *actually achieve* efficiencies that are competitive relative to other producers—domestic and foreign. Efficiency requires responsive investment mechanisms, dynamic business start-up and closure mechanisms, and efficient labor and resource allocation.

But efficiency is not the end-all. The overarching purpose of a legitimate economic system is to maximize the developmental opportunities, the safety, the security, the comfort, the self-respect, and the creative inspiration of all persons working and living under that system.

For the system to work requires that people *want* to work: that people are inspired enough and loyal enough to give themselves to the task at hand. This means fulfilling the workers' needs for security, respect, creativity, variety. Top management knows this intuitively when setting wages and benefits and working conditions for themselves, but the same considerations seldom extend to the custodians. The security and respect needed by the human psyche are closely linked with what people are paid, including what people are paid *relative* to those around them. Time clocks and production quotas and authoritarian threats can extract obedience, but they do not draw out a person's full energy and initiative and loyalty.

Productivity at the levels now evident in industrialized nations can, by a wide margin, free the citizens of these nations from want, but only if the benefits of that productivity are equitably shared.

Cheap labor is not good for business.

Business entities, and businesspersons as individuals, are harmed by cheap labor (underpaid workers) in many ways. As abundantly discussed, businesses pay heavily (through taxes) to clean up after the bad behaviors of the poverty culture and the underculture. Businesses as well pay out large sums for private security and property insurance to protect themselves from crime.

But businesses lose the most because they cannot sell their goods and services to tens of millions of worker/consumers—those who, at present, do not have the purchasing power to buy what business makes. Cheap labor does not *lead to* impoverished consumers; cheap labor *is* impoverished consumers. It does not matter whether a business produces tennis racquets or milling machines. Even businesses that cater exclusively to the rich need to recognize that their workers are their customers indirectly. Every dollar earned and spent domestically will be re-spent several times over the course of a year, creating more prosperity and more customers and more aggregate demand. This general, aggregate prosperity creates more revenue for all businesses.

Business owners and managers who pay low wages poison their firms' management/labor relationships. In these firms the loyalty and energy of the lowest-paid workers is diminished—or turns into outright hostility. The rate of turnover and firing of low-paid workers is monstrously high. At some level of turnover, employers will no longer invest in the career development of their low-wage workers because of the near-certainty of losing them. Employers cut all possible employee-related costs by simplifying the work so that little training is required, by stripping employees of health insurance, by reducing vacation time, by creating part-time positions, and by outsourcing. All of this breeds further resentment and further erodes loyalty and productivity. Employees leave at their first opportunity—and the circle goes 'round.

Paying workers less than it costs to live is a fool's bargain in the long run.

Appendix One: (continued)

A New Form of Minimum Wage

Our first order of business is to get enough money into the hands of the lowest-paid workers that they may live comfortably and provide their children with an excellent education and a healthy array of developmental opportunities. This, through work at good wages, not through low-paying work supplemented with welfare and transfer programs.

The minimum wage is the most politically palatable and politically familiar tool to raise the lowest wages. The use of the minimum wage is such a time-worn strategy that it feels timid, if not cowardly, to commend it as the centerpiece of any meaningful economic "reform." However, the minimum wage is not as benign as it first appears. If pushed high enough, or allowed to fall too far behind inflation, the associated benefits and consequences are substantial and quick in coming.

Several modifications to the minimum wage structure are recommended. The first modification focuses upon the markedly different income needs between two groups of workers: adults and in-school teens. Different minimum wage levels are recommended for these groups.

Why?

Adults with children need the full-cost-of-living wage detailed in chapter three which identifies the full cost of family responsibility—about $15 per hour (for both parents) in 2003 dollars. Every parent, single or married, needs this level of wage immediately, if not desperately.

In-school teens living at home have markedly lower income needs. In-school teens working for pocket money can generally get by on the current federal minimum wage of $5.15 per hour. But they do have a pressing need for employment opportunities and for community service opportunities. Employment and community service are valuable, perhaps necessary, socialization experiences. Many more teen jobs are needed, and maintaining a lower minimum wage for teens will help increase the number of jobs open to them. It might prove to be good public policy to specifically exclude high school dropouts from eligibility for the adult minimum wage, applying pressure on them to complete school or to get their GED.

(A lower minimum wage for teens, in tandem with a significantly higher minimum wage for adults will mean fewer jobs for adult workers—unless something is done to offset the loss. Permit me to respond to this difficulty in a moment.)

It might also be tempting to establish one minimum wage level for adults *with* children, and another wage level for adults *without* children. It seems sensible on the basis of need, but it is not workable. Different minimum wages for similarly skilled groups of adults would put them in direct wage competition with one another for jobs. Employers would, other factors being equal, prefer the single adult if that person could be hired more cheaply, even though adults with children carry the heaviest financial burdens and probably need the work most.

The potential wage/job competition between adults and teens can be managed through definitions and restrictions. Restrictions on hours, as now apply to most work-study and summer job programs, would help emphasize a scholastic focus for teens. Limiting the number of hours a teen could work, and restricting full-time work to the summer months, would make it more difficult for businesses to base their profitability on the use of teen labor. Some businesses will, inevitably, shift some work from adults to teens, but many sociological factors will limit the hiring of teens. Most businesses prefer to keep production operations that require judgment or clear communications or attention to safety in the hands of adult workers. Most customers prefer to conduct business transactions with adults because customers prefer maturity and experience; businesses will continue to prefer adults for these positions. As well, most parents want to limit the work hours of their teens when they are in school.

Teens who have moved out of the family home, even those with children, may be best served by a low minimum wage, supplemented by social service programs. Permitting a higher minimum wage for teens living outside the home of their immediate families might create an inappropriately attractive incentive for teens to move out prematurely.

Other special accommodations might also accompany the new minimum wages.

New immigrants who are on the citizenship track need special accommodation. New immigrants commonly find themselves sitting on the sidelines of the economy and forced onto welfare. It could be argued that employers who hire new immigrants deserve some modest financial reward for opening their doors to this often-hard-to-employ group. Employers might be required to pay new adult immigrants the full adult minimum wage; the employer would then be subsidized, say, $3 per hour for the first six months to a year that the new immigrant is on the job. This subsidy should approximate the actual per-hour cost of integrating that new immigrant into the business. Time limits would be set on how long after their initial employment new immigrants would be eligible for subsidized wages. The employer could be required to commit to six months of continued employment at the full-cost-of-living minimum wage *after* the subsidy is discontinued. This requirement would help exclude from the subsidy program employers who did not have an earnest interest in training *and keeping* these new immigrants on the payroll. The additional governmental oversight that would come part and parcel with public subsidization of private work would make it more difficult for employers to utilize illegal immigrants.

The point is to get immigrants established in a good job, to have the economic system capture their productivity, to get them off public assistance and empowered by their own economic independence—to make them taxpayers, not tax takers.

The mentally and physically handicapped also require unique accommodation.

When handicapped persons can work, they usually want to work. The economy, for efficiency if for no other reason, needs to more fully embrace their creativity and productivity.

The handicapped, if living independently, need a full-cost-of-living income.

Businesses or agencies that hire handicapped individuals often face extra expenses. Just as businesses that provide work for new immigrants deserve help through wage subsidization, similarly, businesses that supply jobs for the handicapped deserve a reward for their outreach and accommodation. Subsidization is not always necessary; handicapped individuals, working jobs suited to their abilities, can often match the productivity of their non handicapped coworkers.

It is suggested that we subsidize employers to whatever extent is necessary to get them to step forward to offer work to the handicapped. It is simply much better to have these individuals working if they can and if they want to.

Work for the handicapped should include government work if private work cannot be found—never make-work, but respectful and appropriate work that truly needs doing.

Other populations may also need special accommodation.

What about persons who want or need to work part-time? Even with a higher minimum wage, fewer hours means less income. Nothing practical can be done except to set policies that try to insure that everyone who wants to work more hours, can. Part-time work, and poverty itself, is not socially troublesome as long as it is short-term and voluntary, and as long as children's futures are not being jeopardized.

It is recommended that adults and in-school teens be *immediately* given the full dollar amount of the minimum wage determined to be appropriate for their group. Our government has historically raised the minimum wage penny by penny and always lagging inflation. This will not do; it solves nothing. If we raise the minimum wage only slightly for adult workers, they will still be poor, they will still require public assistance, and they will still be plagued by the stresses of poverty. All of the old social problems will persist. Nor must we yield to the political temptation of raising the minimum wage just above the poverty line so as to force people out of means-tested programs yet still not give them a living wage. This would create nothing but more anxiety and anger and bad behavior. It is essential that the wage be raised high enough to meet the full range of family responsibilities. Again, that means at least $15 per hour (2003 dollars)—and that assumes both parents are working and contributing to the families finances. An impossibly optimistic assumption, but we must start somewhere.

The second reason that we need to immediately raise the adult wage to near the $15 level is to achieve the cost saving sociological objectives. We will realize few systemic savings or quality-of-life gains unless we reduce the bad values and behaviors associated with extreme or extended or chronic poverty. We must also acknowledge that it will take some time before the bad values and behaviors now instilled in the underculture can be put behind us.

Once implemented, the minimum wage should be fixed to an inflation index.

This recommendation begs a question so glaring and serious that it needs an answer now: if the minimum wage is raised, most product prices will have to be raised. Does this not set in motion a fruitless inflationary spiral? What is gained?

The question that one is tempted to ask is the wrong question. The wrong question is: how, if the minimum wage is pushed significantly upward, can the price of goods and services be held at approximately their current levels (adjusting over time of course for inflation)? The answer to that question is: they can't. Product prices will go up, and for some items significantly. But this is precisely what needs to happen. In a properly-functioning economic system all costs of production should show up in the price of the product, including the full cost of living for every worker who contributes to that product's production.

It is a curious and approximate truth that in the long run we are better served to pay the full cost of producing a good or service at the time of its purchase. There are many amusing and sobering lessons on this point. Nuclear electrical power is a comically expensive example: we were promised "inexpensive energy," only to be informed later that we would also have to pay for the processing, burying, and safeguarding of millions of tons of radioactive waste for 500,000 years. Refusing to acknowledge the full cost of toxic by-products as part of the cost of the product has ended in the creation of a huge federal Superfund bureaucracy to clean up our national mess. Not paying the full cost of living for the labor in a product also carries a high price. Cheap goods produced by underpaid workers eventually put upon us *even more* than the cost of the labor we did not pay for in the first place; this extra cost, of course, is the sociological cost that falls upon us when the needs and aspirations of the human animal are denied or neglected. We are almost always better off to pay the full cost of a product through the price of that product and at the time of its purchase. The most important cost to include, I argue, is the full cost of living for the human beings that made the product.

The right question to ask is: what is the total dollar-cost out of my pocket that I as a consumer *and taxpayer and homeowner and businessperson* will have to pay for the products and services I buy, when I no longer have to pay for all the poverty that the current rules of the economic game create? And more importantly for our souls and our children: what will be the gains in quality of life and quality of nation compared with what we now have?

There are substantial macroeconomic cost offsets (offsetting the increased prices we will have to pay for goods and service). Some of these cost offsets, although not all, can be realized quickly. Let me list some of them briefly.

1.)   If businesses are compelled by a minimum wage law to pay their lowest-wage workers more, pressure will immediately bear upon businesses to hold down their *total* labor cost. The higher minimum wage will be, to some modest extent, offset by reduced (or frozen) salaries and "total compensation" for the highest paid owners, executives, professionals and technicians. This is the transfer of resources that is most needed—an income transfer from the highest-paid to the lowest-paid.

Owners and top executives, the members of corporate boards of directors, and groups of powerful shareholders, have devised every imaginable stratagem to channel corporate money to their personal enrichment. These executives are not receiving, as they so often claim, what a free labor market rewards them for their talents; they are, rather, taking all they can, all they dare, through salaries and bonuses and stock deals that they and their colleagues have rigged in their own favor through the raw power of their executive positions. They can extract these huge salaries and bonuses and stock options and retirement packages because the people who sign off on these compensation packages are sharing the ride on the same gravy train.

Owners and top executives will accept the redistribution of their income kindly. They will use every means they can think of (wage concession demands, importing, outsourcing, moving production overseas, and others) to retain the current pay structure. For the rich, and for the body politic, this transition will not be pleasant. The unpleasantness associated with pulling the highest incomes downward is precisely the unpleasantness that is necessary to achieve more systemic efficiency and to achieve the income and wealth distribution needed to protect this nation's families and children. Fortunately, as a political matter, the individuals who will lose income are wholly within the top 5 percent of earners; almost everyone in the bottom 40 percent of the population will be helped.

As mentioned, businesses' other alternative (instead of reducing compensation at the top) is to try to tap into cheap foreign labor by contracting out work (outsourcing) or by moving their production operations overseas. The cheap-foreign-labor dilemma will be discussed in the "Trade and Globalization" section.

2.)   Raising the minimum wage to the level suggested (to about $15 per hour in 2003 dollars) will *automatically* eliminate all workers who receive this wage from eligibility for all means-tested welfare and transfer programs. Taxpayers will *automatically* pay less for welfare and transfer programs. Taxpayers will also pay less, or not at all, for all public services now provided primarily for to the poor—particularly healthcare services. Some immediate savings would also be realized relative to the cost of police, courts, prisons, drug rehab, and more; but most of these saving would be realized slowly over a decade or two as the bad values and behaviors of the poverty culture and underculture fade.

The potential savings are enormous. Every extra police officer (extra, that is, above and beyond the number of police that would be needed if we were not dealing with poverty), every extra prison guard, every extra drug rehab councelor, every extra doctor and nurse needed because of poverty adds to our tax bill; every private security guard, every electronic alarm system, every security light, every fence, every padlock, every act of theft and vandalism adds to the cost of the products we buy. In ten to twenty years the savings could easily approach two trillion dollars *per year* in an 11.5 trillion dollar economy (2003 dollars, compared to 2003 GDP). Still, in the first three to five years following implementation of a significantly higher minimum wage, it is certain that the savings from reduced welfare and reduced public services alone will not be enough to offset the higher prices we will have to pay for goods and services.

3.)   As welfare recipients are turned into workers (into government workers if necessary) and as poorly-paid workers are turned into well-paid workers, instead of formerly-poor individuals drawing tax dollars out of the public till, they will instead be paying taxes into the public till. This is a double gain to the favor of all taxpayers. Turning the poor into taxpayers will spread a greatly reduced tax burden over literally tens-of-millions of new taxpayers. But less demand for public assistance will not automatically translate into lower taxes; government agencies will desperately cling to their money and public administrators to their jobs. Laws will be needed to enforce a linkage between reduced welfare and transfer expenditures, on the one hand, and reduced tax collections on the other.

4.)   The wealthy should continue to be progressively taxed for those welfare and transfer programs that will still be necessary. Progressive taxation will be needed to augment, that is, increase, the amount of income and wealth transferred from the rich to the lowest-income citizens. Wealth needs to be transferred from the top to the bottom even more than does income. Much more aggressive wealth taxation strategies should be considered for individuals with net worth over, say, two million dollars in 2003 dollars. The revenues from progressive wealth and income taxes might be transferred to the lower economic classes through the funding of government jobs or public subsidization of private wages or educational financial aid or on-the-job training or to bolster the Social Security Trust Fund.

Seeing the Savings and Offsets

It is politically essential that every citizen, as a worker and a taxpayer, personally experience these savings and offsets—and quickly. Middle- and lower-class taxpayers will need to pay less taxes—reduced tax rates that closely approximate reduced welfare and transfer payments and public services (police, prisons, etc). This realization of savings must be immediate and substantial and visible. This is vital because the higher cost of goods will bear down on all of us instantly and painfully.

Let me remind the reader again that increasing the minimum wage comfortably above the poverty line provides taxpayers with a critically necessary political assurance: the formerly-poor workers will *automatically* become ineligible for all means-tested programs, and formerly-poor workers will *automatically* become taxpayers instead of tax takers.

It would be economically ideal to elevate everyone—and I do mean everyone—out of poverty (through work at sufficient pay) so that most transfer programs could be eliminated—perhaps 80 to 90 percent or more. Much of this reduction will come from the huge and *automatic* reductions that will result when formerly-poor individuals lose their eligibility for Medicaid. Well-paid workers could afford, and would be expected to carry—and might be required to carry (if they had children)—private health insurance (or to participate in whatever health care coverage scheme the nation comes up with).

A substantial part of the potential social services savings will not be realized until the underculture and their children are socialized in a more prosperous and gentler environment. However, some antisocial behaviors *will* stop, and quickly. When poor families finally escape poverty (this escape is typically facilitated with nothing more—or less—than a stable, good-paying job), they almost instantly move to a better and safer neighborhood, buy a better car and better furniture, give the kids a merrier Christmas, and mow their lawn with regularity. But some bad behavior will persist and we must stand ready to pay for it. This transition will very likely require deficit spending to smooth out the peaks and valleys in the national funds flow.

The Small Business Situation

The notion of shunting some of the owners' and managers' and technocrats' salaries down to the lowest-paid workers is a ludicrous notion for many small businesses. Small business owners and managers and technical personnel often do not, and cannot, extract large incomes for themselves. Often, the revenue or profitability simply isn't there. Some small business owners make less than their employees. How could small businesses cope with the pressures created by a significant rise in the minimum wage?

Small businesses will have no choice but to raise prices (large businesses will also have to raise prices, of course). For some small businesses it is regrettably true that price increases could mean bankruptcy. But for the overwhelming majority it will not. About 90 percent of small businesses serve localized markets—businesses such as restaurants, retailers, car dealers, carpenters, plumbers and on and on. They compete only against other local businesses. If all similar businesses in the local market face the same labor cost structure (a higher *federal* minimum wage), their relative price-competitiveness will not be changed. By and large these small businesses will retain their market share. Both their costs and their revenues will go up.

Higher prices will drive away some of the more price-sensitive customers. But the sales lost to price increases would be offset, in part or in total, by the sales created by having tens of millions of new, better paid worker/consumers in the marketplace. Almost all businesses marketing middle-class goods and services should experience sales volume increases. Remember, about 20 million individuals who are now able to buy only bare necessities will enter the market with *significantly* increased purchasing power. About 20 million *additional* individuals will have *modestly* increased purchasing power.

Further, a great many businesses, large and small, do not compete directly with foreign imports. They have niche products that are unique ("differentiated" is the economist's jargon), or do not easily lend themselves to international trade. Foods that are prepared or refrigerated or frozen are examples, as are fragile or bulky or heavy products. For U.S. producers that do not compete with foreign goods (yet), a federal minimum wage will leave the *relative* price-competitiveness between *domestic* producers unchanged. Market shares would remain fairly stable. These companies also, to the extent that they are producing middle-class goods and services, will experience sales volume increases because so many more millions of people will be able to buy. The rich, although still rich, will be purchasing fewer luxury goods.

For domestic producers that compete directly against goods or services produced by cheap foreign labor, the future is more troubled. This brings us to trade and globalization.

Appendix One: (continued)

Trade and Globalization

Trade opens tremendous opportunities for market growth, new products and better prices. In the long run, free trade and globalization will lead to more economic efficiency and stronger incentives for international cooperation and stability. In the long run free trade is for the good of all. Mutually beneficial trading partnerships foster international understanding, friendship and peace.

That said, fast paced and freewheeling economic globalization is playing havoc with cultures, rich and poor. The differences in wage levels and technology between the developed and developing world are so great, the change so rapid, and the economic dislocations so jarring that neither business, labor nor governments can comfortably and efficiently adjust.

The allure of enormous markets and enormous profits is simply irresistible. So far, trade has been dominated by the largest corporations. For hundreds of thousands of small and medium-sized businesses in developed nations, inexpensive imports have meant contraction or outright bankruptcy. The price paid by the United States has been colossal: manufacturing business closures by the hundreds of thousands, the loss of at least two million manufacturing jobs so far, almost thirty years of losses in real income for our nation's poorest workers, the rise of a whole new class of working poor, and a plague of poverty-related social problems.

As recently as the mid-1980s, our superior technology, mechanization, management and infrastructure, taken together, could offset much of the advantage of cheap foreign labor. This is true now for only a few products and sectors.

In some product sectors, developing nations cannot compete with the computerization and mechanization of the developed nations. In some product sectors, developed nations cannot compete with developing nations on labor-intensive production. These are comparative advantages that nations on both sides of importing and exporting can benefit from if other overriding and overwhelming external costs (inefficiencies) do not offset them. But that is precisely what is happening on all sides: the gains of comparative advantage are being lost to systemic inefficiencies, to business closures and labor dislocations and to the poverty that follows. Small producers and workers in importing and exporting nations alike are being crushed in the pell-mell rush of multinational corporations to grasp market share and to cash in on their technological advantage and cheap labor.

The grasping for competitive advantage can be everywhere seen: grossly imbalanced trade relationships, unbridled marketeering based on raw corporate power, "dumping" goods at below cost, the widespread use of sweatshops and child labor, flooding markets with goods, the distortion of prices through national subsidization and price supports, and the rapid infusions and the abrupt, near-instantaneous extractions of capital. All of it is causing trouble for cultures rich and poor.

There is a national security concern in all of this. Trade and globalization link the economic fate of the United States with the fate of the economies of our trading partners. As our exposure to unstable foreign economies increases, booming and busting economies around the world surge us forward, then throw us backwards. Both the forward surges and the fallbacks impose system inefficiencies. These economies may be nations or regions or trading blocks. The bigger the economy of our trading partner—the nation, the region, the block—the greater the threat that our economy will be pulled down by the recessions and depressions and monetary crises and political upheavals of those partners. The volume of trade for the United States is reaching such a level that we cannot control, or counterbalance, foreign economic and political upheavals through domestic counter-cyclical policies.

U.S. businesses of all sizes, threatened by imports made by cheap foreign labor, have demanded wage and benefit concessions from their workers by threatening to outsource or close or move their operations overseas. This has been checkmate for unskilled and semiskilled workers, and will be for many white collar workers also. Many corporations have been able to say to labor, "Take the wage we offer or we will eliminate your jobs." U.S. workers have been, and will continue to be, forced to accept lower wages and reduced benefits and layoffs and longer bouts of unemployment. Government, of course, is left to mop up the social mess that unemployment and poverty leaves behind.

Even *skilled* U.S. workers cannot compete against their skilled foreign counterparts, who work for small fractions of the United States' median wage. The shifting of computer programming and accounting and tele-servicing work to other countries is only the beginning of a trend to move white collar jobs overseas.

And there is no end to the phalanxes of cheap labor ready and desperate to take the business and the jobs from developed nations. As many as five-hundred million Chinese are lined up; then there is India and Malaysia and Indonesia, then Central America, then much of South America and all of Africa. There is no way the American economy can outwait this trend.

Without regulation and structural change, millions of American jobs (and jobs in all developed-nations) will be displaced by cheap foreign labor. It is fair to say that U.S. businesses have barely begun their strategic use of outsourcing and offshore production. For the sake of retaining our businesses and sustaining our workers, we cannot prudently leave our future to the forces of the current regime of international trade and labor markets.

Permit me to say this bluntly: the combination of quick and abundant capitalization, state-of-the-art production machinery, aggressive management, and cheap labor (as is now present in several Asian nations) is checkmate for many businesses and workers in developed nations. The nations that get the jobs and do the production and control production technology (taking the profits and the economic surpluses that flow from mass production) will soon also take the lead in research and development and innovation. Japan is already a leading innovator in all aspects of computer design, production methods, auto design and machine tools.

We must not forsake our small and medium-sized businesses, nor our workers, to a trade system that is almost solely to the advantage of a handful of huge multinational manufacturing and trading corporations. To do so will mean more bankrupt businesses, more unemployed citizens and more poverty. It will mean fewer U.S. consumers with discretionary purchasing power to buy what U.S. businesses produce.

I know very well that many of my conservative colleagues find satisfaction in having labor on its knees in a take-it-or-leave-it position. For some businessmen who have come to loath labor through their dealings with unions, this is a dream come true. However, if we look objectively at the lost business revenues and the business bankruptcies and the lower wages and lower benefits, it has been a nightmare for business and labor and the nation.

Under the current trade regime there have been few winners other than the large multinational corporations. It is often claimed that consumers have benefited from the lower prices. This is true, but only in the perverse sense that lower prices have come hand in hand with lower wages, and millions more poor people. Although inflation for goods and services has been held to 1 to 4 percent, real wages for the lowest-paid workers have dropped about 10 percent over the past thirty years.

Any joy that business owners and managers might glean from watching labor be forced into accepting lower wages should be chastened by concern for the future of their own businesses. Hundreds of thousands of businesses over the past thirty years have met their final fate because of the unbridled competition with cheap imports and because tens-of-millions of would-be customers (U.S. consumers) have lost their purchasing power. Our middle class is rapidly dividing into a few tens of thousands who rise to affluence and tens of millions who slide into, or to the edge of, poverty.

These tens of millions are the customers that business needs, but business must first pay these workers/consumers enough to buy what business produces.

What might be done?

Two fundamental responses are called for:

The first challenge is to deal with the huge wage differentials between developed and developing nations.

Raising the minimum wage to the levels I have recommended will quickly threaten U.S. competitiveness in international trade. In the long run, given time to focus and improve our productivity, there is much we can do to compete. In the short term our options are severely limited.

I advocate prudent protectionism and aggressive management of trade—multilateral if possible, unilateral if necessary.

I can feel the writhing of conservatives alive and dead.

My conservative friends, let us not be ingenuous in our outbursts demanding "free trade:" it is a time-honored tradition for staunchly conservative CEOs to beg, bribe, scare and threaten Congress and the President in order to get tariff protection. When it is *their* product or *their* industry or *their* job at stake, conservative businesspersons see protectionism as right, fair and patriotic. They all claim systemic problems beyond their control—and in most cases correctly so. When in crisis, a business wants active government. Businesses ask for targeted tax relief or loans or bailouts; buy-ups of surplus production, price supports or direct subsidization. To the extent that the playing field is unfairly tilted against them, business should ask for and receive help.

Just as good business management is measured by its control over the business' interrelated systems, so should good, prudent macroeconomic management be measured by the degree to which we compel our economic system into the service of the nation and all of its citizens. Trade, like any business, needs good management. The political left has claimed the slogan "fair trade, not free trade." "Fair" is what business and labor should demand, just as corporate executives demand fairness when pleading for tariff protection.

It is not fair for American businesses to face price competition from foreign businesses that pay their workers a tiny fraction of what U.S. businesses must pay their workers to live decently. And it is not fair for American workers and their children to be forced into poverty despite their earnest effort and frugality.

Legitimate economic and political systems in all nations are obliged to regulate the pace of trade and the commodities being traded when their cultures and economies are being gravely harmed.

It is recommended that tariffs, when deemed necessary, be set at levels that attempt to split down the middle the comparative advantage between the trading partners. In some cases the primary criteria would be the relative labor cost advantage—a Labor Cost Differential Tariff, if you will. In other cases the criteria would be relative technological advantage. This gives the cheap-labor nation *some* continuing labor-cost advantage, allowing them to attract sales and investment. Setting the tariff at the middle point also keeps efficiency pressures on rich-nation producers. The tariff should be set so that superior technology, automation, management, and infrastructure of rich-nation producers stand a fighting chance against cheap labor, and also so that intensive labor stands a chance against mechanization.

When the difference in comparative advantage between two trading nations is reduced, the wage- and technology-focused tariffs would be reduced, opening up more, and freer, trade.

The answer to the large international wage differentials is not, as U.S. business might prefer to think, to let U.S. wages be pulled down. It is simply not socially or politically acceptable to cut U.S. wages enough to be competitive with those in developing nations. It would mean riot at the very least.

Sufficient, comfortable wages are for business' good every bit as much as for labor's. To the extent that U.S. business depends on U.S. domestic sales (about 90 percent of U.S. business output is domestically consumed, not exported), so does it depend on U.S. worker/consumer purchasing power.

Additionally, our trade policy should insist upon elevating the wages of foreign workers, helping to usher the developing world into prosperity, while at the same time relieving our businesses and our workers of the anxiety and turmoil caused by the international wage and price imbalances. There are many mechanisms to do so, but the most compelling pressure we can apply is simply to demand that foreign contractors who produce goods for our consumption pay wages comfortably above the minimum wage in their country. U.S. corporations operating overseas could reasonably be compelled to pay, say, 25 to 50 percent above the prevailing minimum wage of the region or country in which they were operating. They can easily afford to do so.

And this is the best part: if U.S. corporations paid a markedly better wage in the overseas factories they own (or control through production contracts), U.S. corporations, and the United States as a nation, would become international heroes, welcomed by the general populations wherever they operate, instead of being regarded everywhere by the general populations as exploiters and profiteers. There is no reason that U.S. business, when it takes its factories overseas, should be The Ugly, Greedy American. The U.S. corporate presence in foreign nations has ambassadorial and national security components that should not be sacrificed to squeezing the last penny of profit out of a foreign worker or a foreign nation.

Secondly, all nations need to limit their overall exposure to international markets. Few nations will do so, but that is all the more reason for the United States to do so. For each nation, trade exposure needs to be small enough that that nation's anti-recession policies and resource-capacity can effectively counterbalance the effect when their trading partners fall into recession or depression. This protection can never be absolute, but every nation needs to retain substantial control over its economic destiny, over its domestic economic foundation.

This is especially true for the United States. We have too much to lose to bet our economic stability on the stability of developing nations. In a world that has not found an answer to the business cycle or war, too much economic interdependence is imprudent. Interdependence will come certainly, and all too quickly, no matter what we do. We must, I think, as a national economic policy, resist overexposure to trade, even though it means our multinational corporations will have to give up some market share. Slower and steadier growth is better. It will better serve the world, our nation, the multinationals and labor. It is suggested that we trade some growth and market share for substantial control of our economic future.

How can a limit on trade exposure be enforced?

Corporations, consistent with their missions, will aggressively reach for market share. Government power and will are increasingly co-opted and dwarfed by corporate power and will. Government's regulatory institutions struggle and equivocate under the complexity and uncertainty; the corporate purpose is focused and clear. However, government—public policy—needs to guide the pace and direction of trade to safeguard our national security and economic stability. The freight train of "free trade" will run away with us if we let it. It is running away with us at this moment. A pleasant, self-regulating market-based answer to moderating the speed of globalization and balancing the labor-cost differentials between nations is not apparent. I regret to conclude that government regulation, through multilateral agreements when possible but unilateral action when necessary, seems the right and the pragmatic and the only course.

Developed and developing nations have little choice: both sides should and must protect their economies and cultures from those components of trade that threaten their businesses, workers and social fabric. The United States must protect its economy, not wholly, but prudently, from the world's political upheavals and economic recessions.

Let us look at the United States specifically. I would humbly suggest that the percentage of our gross national product that is exported and imported needs to be limited. If our total exports and imports were 5 percent of our GDP, international recessions would pull down our economy only slightly. If our total exports and imports were 25 percent of our GDP, sagging exports almost certainly would pull the United States into recession. (Our exports (1.019 trillion) and imports (1.508 trillion) now hover around 22.5 percent of our 11.25 trillion GDP (2003). Exports are about 9 percent of GDP.)

I do not claim to know the right number. Econometric models can estimate the impact at different levels of trade exposure. Precision is not required, and incremental experimentation to find the prudent level of exposure is possible.

I will leave the matter here.

Appendix One: (continued)

Recession Avoidance and Management

A higher minimum wage does not mean much to a person without a job. For most poor persons, there is, quite literally, nothing between them and poverty but a good job at a good wage. At this time (2004), 130,000 to 140,000 new jobs must be created each month to absorb our expanding population. Our ability to avoid recessions, or minimize their duration, has a substantial impact on economic growth rate.

My scheme imposes a new problem. If the minimum wage is raised significantly, companies will become increasingly reluctant to hire unskilled and semi-skilled labor. If the minimum wage were raised as high as it must be to provide a comfortable living wage, then not only must economic growth keep up with population growth, but growth will need to create enough labor demand that business and government will continue to hire at sufficient rates so that full employment is reached and maintained.

Can our system grow fast enough?

Western-style capitalism is by its nature a growth model. Absorbing the growing U.S. population, and reabsorbing the workers that some employers will layoff when the minimum wage is raised, requires an annual growth rate of about 2.5 percent. That represents about 1.2 percentage points of growth to absorb new entries into the workforce, and about 1.3 points of growth to re-absorb workers laid off by businesses that could not adjust to the new minimum wage. Historically, in a stable economy, we have routinely achieved growth rates between 3 and 6 percent, and very much higher rates of growth are possible if we are willing to accept macroeconomic actions to control inflation. (Some economists argue that rapid growth is the last thing our nation and world need. They suggest, among other things, that the existing work can be shared more broadly by having a shorter work week. This will work, but with its own consequences.)

Sufficient growth is easily possible if we can get control of recessions. Recessions delay entrepreneurial initiative and create a fear of uncertainly for consumers, producers and financiers. Every recession bankrupts tens of thousands of businesses. The national and personal financial losses of even a mild recession are appalling, and, of course, represent system inefficiencies in addition to the cost of poverty. The uncertainties created by recession loop back on themselves to create fear even when the statistics do not warrant it. Indeed, thwarting the onset of the *psychology* of recession is central to solving the riddle of recession.

Sustained growth requires that the impact of the business cycle be minimized. Poverty cannot be significantly reduced until the frequency and duration of business cycles are reduced.

Recessions have vexed economists and politicians. Eliminating recessions may prove impossible, but reducing the length and severity of recessions can be done with a more aggressive application of familiar macroeconomic management tools.

What causes recession? Fundamentally, recessions occur when individual consumer confidence drops because a sufficient mass of people are fearful for their financial futures. People slow their buying, and a downward spiral of reduced business revenues and layoffs and more consumer fear follow. Consumer confidence can be weakened by anything, domestic or foreign, that signals uncertainty.

Catastrophic recession—depression—occurs when the uncertainties of the typical recession are deepened by high levels of personal and corporate debt. When consumers and businesses, faced with unemployment and reduced revenue, suddenly can no longer carry their debt, the wave of insolvency and bankruptcy that follows dramatically escalates anxiety in both the financial community and in the general population. When individuals or businesses are carrying levels of debt at or near their fiscal capacity, the economy becomes a house of cards; the higher this house is, the more unstable it is, and the greater the personal and national trauma when it comes down.

Individual consumer confidence, it is suggested, is the crux of recession avoidance and recovery.

You will notice that I have associated recession only with *individual consumers*, not with business or governmental economic activity. All business and government consumption, in the end, translates into individual consumption. A business may sell only to other businesses, but eventually a product or service is produced for individuals. Governments "sell" a few goods and services to businesses, and many to individuals, often whether we want them or not. In the end, individuals buy everything, whether a baseball bat or an industrial press or a locomotive or a submarine.

Individual consumer confidence has three primary components.

First, consumer confidence—our confidence—rests upon our perception of the security and sufficiency of our income. Is our job secure? If we lose our job, do we believe we can get back on our feet quickly? Do we believe that The System stands ready to assist us and to assist the recovery of the economy? Or do we view recession as some sort of act of god beyond our control? Our view of the matter determines how quickly we circle our financial wagons, how quickly we reduce our spending.

Second, our confidence as consumers rests upon the adequacy and safety of our savings and investments. High levels of volatility in the stock and bond markets or sustained loses in our personal investments quickly unnerve us, even if we have a good job.

Third, consumer confidence rests upon the consumer's faith in the stability and safety of his or her community and nation and world. Any real or imagined danger, or any social change that threatens our personal or national stability, will put us on guard. International instability—war or foreign depressions or international monetary crises—weakens consumer confidence by destabilizing the financial markets. Terrorism is an extreme example, but currently very real and present. We are currently steeling our nerves against what will happen to our economy and political order if we are attacked on a catastrophic scale.

Globalization has forced the U.S. economy to share the economic fate (sometimes good and sometimes bad) of other nations and regions and trading blocks. Some consumers, in their concurrent role as laborers, understand personally the threat of cheap foreign labor to their jobs and wages. All of this breeds wariness and restraint in spending.

If we were totally isolated from the international economy, and if every citizen in our nation kept spending at a steady pace (at their typical level during good economic times), national recessions would not occur. That sound like overstatement, but it is not.

Let us, for a couple of paragraphs, pretend that international uncertainties do not exist, and consider only the domestic side of things.

Consumer confidence requires that every worker's income be protected, and with a considerable degree of certitude. This fundamentally means that both income *and work* need some measure of protection. Two elements must be present to provide this protection: a strong job market for workers to turn to, and a strong and evident safety net.

In the United States, income protection has historically come from a combination of unemployment insurance and welfare. The problem with unemployment insurance and welfare is that they do not come anywhere near to replacing the lost income from a lost job. Both unemployment insurance and welfare *drastically* reduce an individual's income, requiring that person or family to immediately and deeply reduce spending.

Personal savings help a little to brace up confidence, but most low-income workers have no savings whatever, and few people have enough savings to outlast a recession. Nor does the availability of some savings offset the psychological impact of losing one's income flow. When citizens see their savings evaporate under the heat of basic living expenses, their anxiety rises exponentially. They stop every cent of nonessential spending.

Not only must personal income be protected, *but, much more importantly, it must be protected quickly.* I suggest a FEMA (Federal Emergency Management Administration) model and mentality: rapid, preplanned, orderly response. Just as FEMA responds to localized disasters, so must anti-recession policy respond quickly to localized economic crises. Make no mistake: when a major employer closes down in a community, it can be a disaster for that community and is a disaster in fact for the laid off workers and their families. Immediate, aggressive, localized responses to localized layoffs and business closures, I believe, can avert most *national* recessions if the response takes the correct form.

Speed of response is critical, not only to reduce the personal and communal impact of layoffs or closures but also to prevent the crystallization of a regional or national recession psychology. When citizens believe that recession is imminent, their belief becomes self-fulfilling; they curtail spending. Our goal must be to aggressively prevent the personal and localized business crises that instill fear.

Workers/consumers need to know that an effective local and national response system stands ready. We need to know that The System will not strip us of our income and savings, that we will not be forced to default on family responsibilities, and that we will not have to give up too much of our lifestyle.

Does this not require large public expenditures? Yes, but recession, if left to run its traditional course, also requires massive public expenditures in the form of unemployment insurance payouts, in welfare and more transfer payments, and in greater demand for public services such as police and prisons. A typical recession can run anywhere from two to five years—and occasionally longer. Current policy has us making bare-subsistence stipends to millions of persons throughout long recessions. I propose larger stipends, precisely targeted, and quickly provided—but for much shorter periods of time. Again, the object is to stop the psychology of recession from taking hold—locally, regionally, nationally.

It is always better, I suggest, to provide work as opposed to unemployment benefits or welfare. If we are going to pay out public money, it should be, to the greatest extent possible, for work done.

Work is almost always better than welfare, even if it is government work. This assumes, of course, that the government work needs to be done and that it will yield a generous (and, ideally, a quantifiable) return on our public investment dollar. There is always plenty of such work if we exert ourselves to identify it.

When a person is laid off or fired or quits, I suggest a two-month transition period during which the unemployed persons either supports themselves out of personal savings or are supported by unemployment benefits at 90 percent (or more) of their former income. If the unemployed person is living out of his or her savings, they may or may not look for work, as they see fit. If the unemployed person chooses to utilize unemployment insurance or public assistance during the transition period, an aggressive search for work would be required of them during the transition period.

At the end of two months, everyone utilizing unemployment insurance or public assistance would be given two choices: to take a private job if they can find one (with government subsidizing the wages in some cases), or take a part- or full-time government Ready Work job.

What do I mean by government Ready Work? These would be public jobs, or subsidized private-sector jobs, that can be *instantly* made available to any job seeker, whether he or she is merely the occasional individual who has quit work or been fired, or is one of a large group of workers who have been laid off because of a business closure. City, county, state and federal governments would create a pri-oritized list of Ready Work jobs.

This work needs to be of all types—manual, clerical, professional. Highway and park maintenance are obvious candidates. Public buildings, schools and other public structures could be repaired or renovated. Professionals might be asked to plan or execute studies on proposed legislation. Professionals might help non-profits or local governments with general administration. Schools can always utilize more tutors and classroom aides. Community health clinics always need extra clerical staff, and sometimes management assistance. Library hours could be expanded where there is demand. Youth recreation centers could be staffed, as could counseling centers for troubled teens. All levels of government typically need help keeping their data bases updated. The key to effective use of the public dollar is to make sure Ready Work yields a return on our public dollar. This can be assured through planning and prioritizing. The return on investment of Ready Work needs to be immediately apparent to taxpayers.

These Ready Work jobs should be identified in advance, valued for return on investment, prioritized according to value, and always instantly available. Ready Work would be for the most part provided either by expanding or accelerating projects or programs that are already in progress or by implementing programs that have been pre-approved specifically for Ready Work (anti-recession) pur-poses.

A federal/state partnership using the current unemployment insurance structure would finance these Ready Work positions, in part or in total, depending on the size and length of the crisis.

Quickness and certainty of response are the key. Acting too late, hesitating to hire the unemployed, will achieve little. Again, the general population must know that The System simply is not going to let individuals and families go without income, or let recession take hold. When that faith is justified by action, families and individuals will continue spending at rates near their normal level.

Ready Work jobs should be good jobs with levels of responsibility and creativity roughly matched to the abilities of the workers who hold them. The workers have a right to be respectfully treated and not stigmatized as welfare recipients; they would not be welfare recipients; they would be temporary public employees. They should be paid the full-cost-of-living minimum wage and be provided with basic health insurance.

Ready Work does not have to be government work. Large and medium-sized employers could be kindly asked (and required if necessary) to identify work that they would hire done if they could receive agreed-upon levels of wage subsidization. Private companies who hold contracts for government work would, perhaps, make ideal partners in such a program.

If a large local employer believes it will have to close its business, a joint public-private review of the situation should be required. We should not permit the pretension that private business is strictly private business; there is a profound *community* interest in the good health and continuance of every private business.

Government assistance to a company that is considering closure might take the form of short-term subsidization of wages to keep the company operating temporarily until a closure or continuation-of-business plan could be formed. No reasoned option should be overlooked to sustain business operations and employment that is warranted by product demand. (Businesses often close operations when demand and profits slump, even though some demand remains. It may be that closure is not warranted, that restructuring to the lower demand is viable. The business may not have a compelling interest in this smaller market, but the employees—and the community—have a powerful interest in retaining the jobs.) These options might include employee stock ownership structures or cooperative employee ownership. Any government partnership with business should not alter the demand-driven, demand-guided direction that restructuring might take. It is the guidance provided by market demand that underlies systemic efficiency. The point is this: the process of downsizing or closure needs to be thought through. Employees deserve a voice in their destiny, and fair warning if closure cannot be avoided. A formal framework needs to be present to investigate new possibilities, new structures, new investment opportunities, all of it focused on keeping and expanding work opportunities thereby stabilizing personal incomes.

Government should play, to the extent possible, a minor and temporary role.

If Ready Work were well-administered, society would benefit by the individual's continuing productivity, by sustaining a cultural work ethic and by keeping the economy going by keeping consumer confidence and spending more stable. Individuals benefit by staying mentally and physically active through work, feeling productive and worthwhile, retaining their dignity as family providers, maintaining human contact (avoiding the isolation that so often grips the unemployed) and keeping communication skills sharp and work habits intact.

Protecting individual income and savings is the strongest antirecession policy and the strongest antipoverty policy.

After the two month transition period, a minimum of part-time (half-day) Ready Work would be required; the other half of the day could be utilized for job search activities. Full-time work should be offered to anyone with children and to anyone who wants full-time work.

How does a government-employed person transition back into private work?

During the transition period, a full array of work-search services would be provided, and work-search obligations would be respectfully enforced upon public assistance recipients. Once a person is hired for a Ready Work job, he or she should keep that job until private work is found. We do not want the individual to be idle, or to be forced to live on an insufficient unemployment stipend supplemented by welfare. Permit me to say again: if it is between welfare or work, work is almost always better—even if that work is government work.

Government and private Ready Work would be funded by the current unemployment taxes, with the program restructured to pay higher monthly benefits for much shorter periods of time. Ready Work would also be funded by emergency general fund appropriations as dictated by the breadth and duration of the local or national situation. I suggest that all the income taxes paid by the workers doing Ready Work be earmarked for immediate and future Ready Work funding. Because the total, systemic dollar-cost of even a short recession is so large, anticyclical employment funding should, when needed, be funded with deficit spending.

Recessions are also worsened when consumers slacken their spending because they fear for their savings and investments. The stock market is particularly troublesome in this regard.

If investors bought only safe investments such as government bonds, the trauma of watching one's wealth evaporate during a stock market downturn would be avoided. But our reason and nature tells us to want more than safety. Alert citizens know that the stock market, on average, outperforms government securities. We balance higher return against safety. There is nothing wrong with this reasoning and sentiment, but it has consequences.

When our exuberance runs up share prices to fifty or more times a company's earnings per share, a reckoning is inevitable for both the investor and the economic system. Every stock market investor loves a stock market run-up, but not everyone can endure (wait out) the correction. The personal shock of watching one's net worth precipitously drop, and watching our country's aggregate wealth fall by trillions, means more anxiety and a deeper, longer recession.

Allow me to broach a novel idea relative to investment security. Why not tie the value of a company's stock to the actual value of the company? What a quaint notion. Why not require that the company's stock value reflect the on-the-books, net asset value of the company, with an approximate, and conservative, add-on for goodwill and growth potential. This basis of value would grow or contract as the business grew or contracted.

Small investors want their investments to represent true value. They want stability and surety, not irrational volatility. Most citizens do not understand stock evaluation fundamentals, nor understand how to do the research. Most of us do not have the time or desire to make a profession of stock portfolio management. We want the actual value of the company to be reflected in its stock value. The average investor does not deserve to be taken on a roller coaster ride, first up into a sham heaven, and then down into a real hell.

National and international instability can also weaken consumer confidence and provoke recession. To comprehensively explain how to manage the economic and political instability of the entire world would require at least three more paragraphs. Let me leave international matters as I have in the chapter on trade and globalization.

At the center of recession avoidance is this: consumers must feel confident that their income and savings are safe. If recessions can be dealt with successfully—some avoided, others managed—we will have gone a long way towards stabilizing growth and averting poverty and all that comes with it.

Appendix One: (continued)

Other Program Components

Even if these proposals worked perfectly and quickly, much would still need to be done around the edges of the central policies.

Healthcare: Every child and every adult needs health protection. The hemorrhage of money lost by using emergency rooms and county hospitals for primary care clinics for the poor should be immediately cauterized. We let politicians convince us that all this "extra" health care would cost the nation a great deal of money that "the nation cannot afford," stupidly-blind to that fact that every day we are spending a fortune on medical care for the poor—twice or three times what health care for the poor would cost if it were provided through the normal, structured channels of insurance or HMOs. We pay dearly through misused and overused emergency room care, through building and staffing huge county hospitals, through building and equipping and staffing community sliding-pay-scale clinics, through Medicaid and Social Security and a hodge-podge of health programs for the poor. Each program carries a large bureaucratic overhead on top of the intrinsic inefficiency of caring for people too little and too late. Not only is neglecting the health care of poor children and adults expensive, it is ethically indefensible.

Schools: All schools need to be adequately funded, and funded with a considerable degree of equality (adjusted for cost-of-service-delivery differences between regions). Private school funding (per student) should be equalized with public school funding, just as we now, in theory, equalize per student expenditures between public schools.

The content of school curriculum is a bit to the side of economics, but permit me these few sentences. Adolescents desperately need and deserve educational and ethical guidance relative to male-female relationships and sexual responsibility. Teens need to understand the consequences of teens having children. They need to know the full range of financial responsibilities that attach to parenthood, that they must be responsible for the children they create, and that their freedom, lifestyle, and career options will be severely truncated by having a child. This is a proper focus of public education, augmenting the role of parents. (Adult parents could benefit from some parent training as well.)

Daycare: If we demand that public assistance recipients work (almost all of them are women with children), then affordable daycare has to be available. Respite childcare is also much needed by frustrated and harried single parents, for the parents' sanity and the children's protection against abuse.

Child protection and development: Funding for child protective services and foster care and adoptive services needs to be, by many professional estimates, at least doubled. It will save us money, and quite quickly. Money invested in children yields a lifetime of productive service and good citizenship is the best possible investment of public money. Children waiting adoption who are difficult to place deserve absolutely whatever public financial support is required to find them families. There is no acceptable reason for these children to languish for years as wards of the state. There are relatively few such children; we can afford to invest heavily in them, and we cannot afford not to invest in them.

Big Brothers, Big Sisters-type mentoring programs need more public support, as does the construction and staffing of boy's and girl's clubs. Providing seed money is often all it takes; communities can—through private and public contributions—self-support many extracurricular activities if they are helped through the initial start up challenges.

Youth employment: Youth jobs, both public and private, need to be assured for our teens. AmeriCorps and Peace Corps type programs provide productive, positive work experience and a sense of pride in country. Many of these positions have a proven return on the investment of the public dollar.

Career education and training: Everything we do to elevate the knowledge and productive capacity of our citizens is good for our economy. Federal and state surveys that project growth or contraction in specific job areas need to be more tightly linked to the availability of financial aid for education and training in those areas. As things now work, the demand for particular skills and professions may, at one moment, fall far short of needed supply. Our educational and training institutions then slowly gear up and start churning out diplomas and certificates, eventually creating a large and lingering oversupply of workers in these areas. Both the shortfall and the oversupply create large inefficiencies. Better future-job-opportunity survey techniques, and better educational and training guidance for incoming students, are needed.

On-the-job training, well designed and administered, is a terrific public investment that precisely matches training to the immediate needs of the participating businesses.

Visiting workers: Immigration, as well as our nation's use of "guest" and "migrant" workers, need to be thoughtfully planned and, in general, limited. Certainly we want, as a generous nation, to help needful workers in other countries and to utilize foreign labor if U.S. workers cannot do the work. But we must put our own house in order first. My conservative friends often tell me that

Americans simply will not do the work that migrant workers do. This is demonstrably not true. Millions of our own citizens would gladly do the manual labor now performed by guest workers if they were paid a dignified wage, a wage sufficient to comfortably support their families. If we can first employ all of our own citizens, and then offer the extra jobs to visiting workers, wonderful. Migrant labor reduces the cost of labor for a few industries, but using migrant workers instead of American workers puts the cost of caring for our own unemployed citizens on the backs of every taxpayer.

Social Security and Medicare: These programs need to be means-tested from top to bottom. These programs transfer tens of billions of dollars every year to the upper middle class and the rich. There is no reason that our Social Security system—at this moment under funded by at least six trillion dollars—should pay benefits to someone with a hundred thousand in annual income from investments and millions in financial assets. The same with Medicare—currently projected to be insolvent by 2019. The wealthy can easily afford top notch private health insurance or pay a full-cost premium into the Medicare system if they prefer. The rich should not consume public dollars so desperately needed by others. All taxes, and particularly FICA taxes, should be progressive. Income-based taxes should be emphasized and regressive taxes summarily reduced and phased out.

Welfare: Every person who received the recommended full-cost-of-living minimum wage (again, about $15 per hour in 2003 dollars) would automatically lose eligibility for public assistance. However, we will still have to assist many of the lagging and troubled children and adults that our neglect and bad policy has already created. Many people will continue to require public help. The full array of services will still have to be made available through public programs—but less of everything.

Representative Democracy: Our campaign finance laws need a bold overhaul. U.S. politicians will not command the trust and respect of the public—that is, earnest respect as opposed to the lugubrious pandering and deference now shown to politicians by favor seekers—until they divorce themselves from the big money of special interests. The United States is a false-democracy; our leadership does not remotely reflect the social or economic demographics of our nation. In the end, with precious few exceptions, our choice is between one rich candidate or another. This plutocracy is so historically persistent, so entrenched, because political power protects economic power, and economic power protects its political benefactors. Not only is our "democracy" structurally illegitimate, it is dysfunctional because poverty leaves so many individuals too meek or too unstable or too angry or too dispirited to participate in politics. No economic change with any meaningful redistributional effect can be sustained until the voices of lower economic classes are heard and respected and counted.

Appendix Two

Statistics on Poverty and Inequality
Current Levels and Historical Trends

Discussing measures of poverty and inequality is like kicking a hornet's nest on a hot day—naked. The ideological swarms come pouring out. Think tanks on the political left and right are busy selecting and omitting data to prove their biases or push their agendas. Statistical chicanery is common.

Government is of some good help here. Government statistical agencies—by shear force of sustained effort, collective judgment, and relentless outside inquisition—have developed a respectable competency and some remarkable databases. Their numbers may not be correct, but they are, by-and-large, close to the mark and comparable over time.

The data that follows is from U.S. Census Bureau, Federal Reserve surveys and Bureau of Labor Statistics reports, unless otherwise noted.

Let us first look at poverty, then income inequality, then wealth inequality.

POVERTY

The official U.S. measure of poverty has been under attack from all sides. Conservatives complain that the U. S. poverty measure is an income-only measure—that wealth is not considered. For example, a family defined as "poor" may still own a house, furniture and car. Some particularly energetic conservatives like to point out that people counted as poor can be millionaires. It is true; a millionaire may be counted as "poor" if their income drops below the poverty line. This is rare, and it does not follow, as some conservatives infer, that millionaires who are mistakenly counted as "poor" then use and abuse public welfare. The wealth holdings of millionaires almost always include liquid financial assets that yield enough income to disqualify them from means-tested assistance. These assertions are broadly untrue and taint other worth conservatives arguments.

Liberals complain that the poverty line is just plain too low and that it is based on an antiquated formula. The Census Bureau, after being vigorously petitioned by academics in the mid-1990s, developed six new Experimental Measures of poverty. Nine other experimental measures have since been added. These measures consider certain types of transfer payments, adjust for various taxes, and include other expenses deemed essential to raising a family. Geographic cost of living differences have also been included in some of the measures. These new measures attempt to more realistically represent the income status of families.

All but one of the new measures indicate higher rates of poverty, in some cases substantially higher.

The traditional U. S. Census Bureau measure of poverty will be used here because it approximates the same rates of poverty as the newer, more comprehensive measures and because this measure is familiar and historically consistent.

GRAPH 1, below, shows the historical pattern of poverty
rates, and the numbers of persons in poverty from 1959 to 2002.

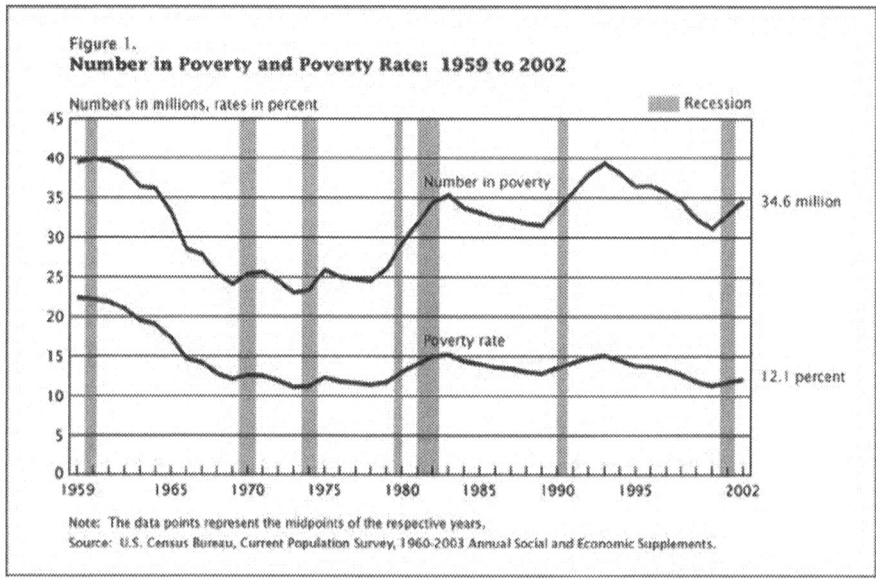

Figure 1.
Number in Poverty and Poverty Rate: 1959 to 2002

Note: The data points represent the midpoints of the respective years.
Source: U.S. Census Bureau, Current Population Survey, 1960-2003 Annual Social and Economic Supplements.

Since 1975 the poverty rate has hovered between about 12 to 15 points. The
poverty rate closely reflects cycles of recession and expansion. Notice that the
poverty rate increases before the official date for the onset of a recession and continues to rise for two or three years after the official end of recession.

Sustained periods of economic growth can reduce poverty dramatically: for
example from 1993 to 2000 the poverty rate went from 15.1 to 11.3—a near all-
time record low. The importance of job steady creation and a tight labor market,
as factors that help reduce poverty, cannot be overemphasized.

The *number of people* in poverty has risen with the population. In 1975, the
official count of persons in poverty was 25.9 million; it is now about 35 million—a 35 percent increase. The rising number of persons in poverty is disturbing because it is from this increasing population of the poor that a
disproportional amount of antisocial and sociopathic and criminal activity arises.

TABLE 1, below, shows the poverty rate for selected groups. For the lay reader, the poverty rate is a percentage; that is, the number of persons in poverty per 100 persons in the specified group.

Poverty Rates for Specified Groups, 2002:
_____

Aggregate groupings:
All persons	12.1	(34,570,000 persons)
All families	9.6	(7,230,000 families)

The racial extremes:
Persons		
White/not Hispanic	8.0	
Black	24.1	
Families		
White/not Hispanic	6.0	
Black	21.4	

Children:
Under 18	15.8	(11,680,000 children)
Under 6	18.5	

The elderly:
Over 65	9.8	The level of dependence on Social
Rate for persons over 65		Security, not to mention Medicare,
if there were no Social		is sobering.
Security	49.0	

The working poor:
Full-time workers	11.5	(Those working a minimum of 035 hours
		per week for 50 weeks, or 1749 hours

The near-poor:
		per year.)
Persons with incomes		
125% over the poverty		
line	16.5	

The ultra-poor:
Persons with incomes		
below 50% of the		
poverty line	4.9	

The effect of
marriage on poverty:
All married couple families	5.6	For married-couple families, not only
White couples	5.3	is the rate or poverty much less than for
Black couples	6.7	"all families", but the Black/White racial
All persons in female-		gap is significantly reduced.
headed households	26.5	
All persons in male-		Compare this single-parent poverty rate
headed households	12.1	with the married rate.

(Source: U.S. Census Bureau, Poverty Tables.)

TABLE 2, below, shows the distribution of the poor by various characteristics for year 2002.

Of all *families* that are poor: (total= 7,230,000 families)

75.0% have children

50.0% are female-headed (no husband present) families
 7.8% are male-headed (no wife present) families
42.2% are married couple families

42.2% are white/not Hispanic families
27.1% are Black families
25.0% are Hispanic families
 3.0% are Asian and other races

Of all *persons* who are poor: (total= 34,570,000 persons)

33.8% are children under 18
55.9% are 18 to 64
10.3% are over 65

45.0% are White/not Hispanic
25.7% are Black
24.7% are Hispanic
 3.6% are Asian or other races

Source: U.S. Census Bureau, Historical Poverty tables

If all federal, state, and local welfare programs (means-tested) were eliminated, about 23% percent of the all persons in the U.S., about one-fourth of our nation's population, would fall below the poverty line.

Income and wealth inequality has increased dramatically, and to near-historic levels, over the last 28 years. Recent changes in the tax code virtually guarantee increasing levels of inequality.

Income Inequality

GRAPH 2, below, shows the changes in various indexes of income inequality since 1975.

(It is not necessary for the casual reader to understand the mathematics and assumptions behind these indexes. Some of these indexes portray a more alarming picture of income inequality; others a more benign picture. These five indexes were selected by the U.S. Census Bureau to broadly characterize income inequality.)

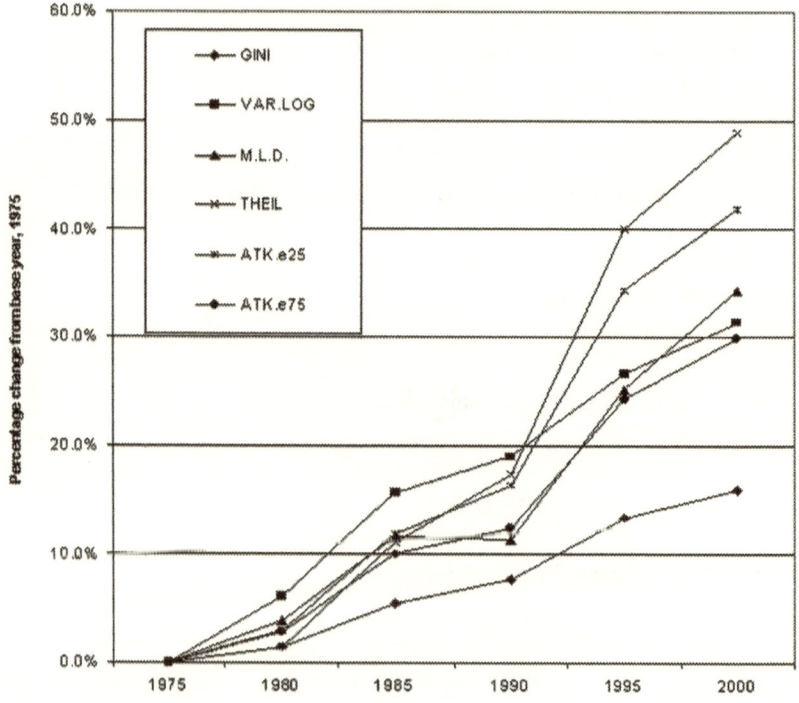

Percentage change in various indexes of inequality for household income, all races, 1975-2002

Each of these indexes shows an historically dramatic increase in income inequality since 1975.

This is in sharp contrast to the period starting in the late 1930's, continuing to about 1978. During this span income inequality slowly decreased and then stabilized.

GRAPH 3, below, shows the percentage change in the share of the nation's total (aggregate) household income received by each quintile (20%) of households since 1975. (Real income; 2002 dollars; all households; all races; base year = 1975.)

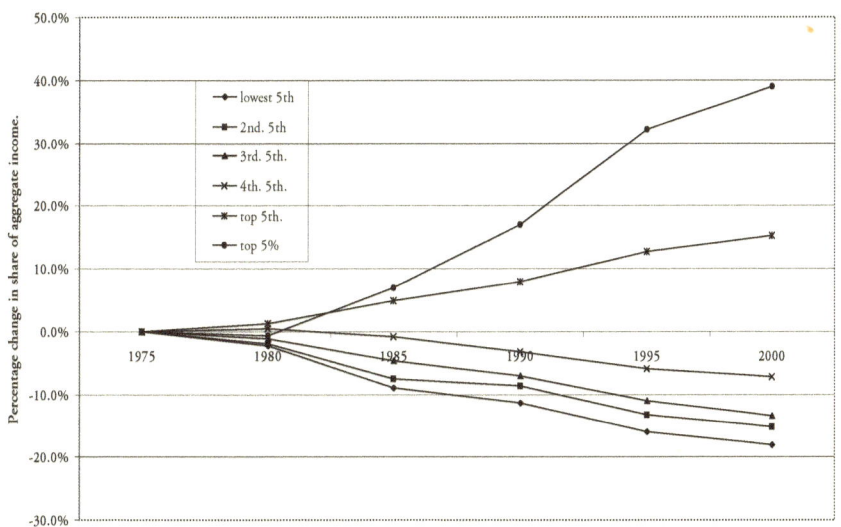

This graph illustrates that:

The bottom 4 quintiles—80 percent of all households—lost income share during this period.

Only the highest-income 20 percent realized any gain in share over this 25 year span—a 17% increase in share.

The highest-income 5 percent of households realized a 38% increase in share.

The highest-income 1 percent (not on graph) of households realized an increase in share of just over 100 percent during this same period.

Shares of Household Income, 2003:

The highest-income 5 percent of households now commands approximately 22 percent of all household income.

The highest-income 20 percent of households now commands about 50 percent of all household income.

The lowest-income 40 percent of households commands about 12.5 percent of all household income.

Average Annual Income for Selected Groups (all races), 2003:

Average income for the highest-income 5% of households: $ 251,010.

Average income for the middle 20% of households: $ 42,802.

Average income for the bottom 20% of households: $ 9,990.

The Racial Gap (emphasizes the extremes), 2002:

Average income for top 5% of white/non-Hispanic households: $ 296,798.

Average income for the top 20% of white households: $ 151,779.

Average income for bottom 20% of black households: $ 5,769.

CEO's Pay as a Multiple of Average Worker Pay, 1960-2001:

GRAPH 4, below, shows the historic relationship between CEO compensation to average worker pay. When calculating CEO compensation, only cashed-in stock options were included.

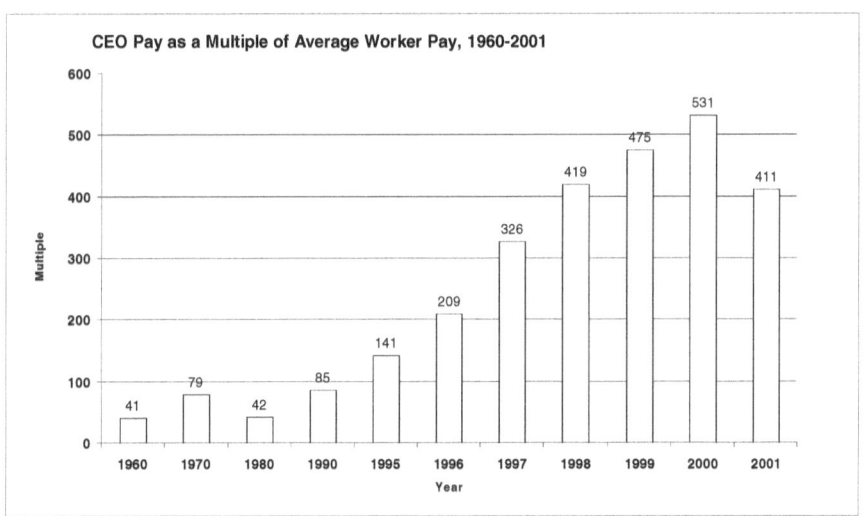

(Sources: *Business Week*, "Annual Survey of Executive Compensation, 2002," canvassing approximately 365 of what *Business Week* defines as "the largest U.S. corporations"; average worker pay is drawn from Bureau of Labor Statistic, Average Weekly Hours of Production Workers and Average Hourly Earnings of Production Workers.)

The average CEO in this 2003 made just under $10 million. That is about 930 times more than a minimum wage worker.

If the minimum wage had risen at the same rate as executive pay since 1990, the minimum wage would now be $21.41 an hour as opposed to the current $5.15 per hour.

If the minimum wage had risen at the same rate as executive pay over the past thirty years it would be about $41.00 (Institute for Policy Studies, 2002 report, "Executive Excess.")

Since reaching its highest real-dollar value in 1968, the minimum wage has lost about 36 percent of its value after adjustment for inflation.

Between 1973 and 2003, real hourly wages of the average American worker fell by about 9 percent. By contrast, from 1947 to 1973, real wages *grew* by 75 percent. (Dr. Edward Wolff, New York University, *The American Prospect*, v12, i3, Feb. 2001.)

One quarter of all workers—about 34 million workers—earn less than $9.00 an hour (2003 dollars). If they worked full time, they would still not reach the poverty line for a family of four in 2003—$18,600. ((Economic Policy Institute, The State of Working America, 2002-2003.)

According to an Internal Revenue Service report on year 2000 earnings, 400 super-rich Americans had a average *annual* income of $174 million each—a combined income of $69 billion.

Liberal economist, Paul Krugman, writing for the *New York Times Magazine*, calculated that in 2003 the 13,000 richest families in the U.S. received as much income as the 20 million poorest families. These wealthy families, on average, have incomes 300 times the average family income.

Wealth Inequality

Wealth is significantly more concentrated than income.

The Federal Reserve's Survey of Consumer Finances found that in 2002 the wealthiest 1 percent of households controls about 33 percent of the nation's private net worth.

The bottom 40 percent of households controls only .3 percent (3/10ths of 1 percent) of privately held net worth. This means that the top 1 percent of households controls about 100 times the combined net worth of the bottom 40 percent of households. The bottom 60 percent of households controls a mere 4.9 percent of the nation's private net worth; the bottom 50% about 2.8 percent. (Federal Reserve data.)

In 1998, the top 1% controlled 38.1 percent. (Edward N. Wolff, "Recent Trends in Wealth Ownership, 1983-1998.") The drop in the stock market through the 2000 recession has disproportionately—and only temporarily—reduced the financial wealth of the rich.) For historical perspective, in 1976, the top 1 percent held about 19% of the nation's private net worth. In other words, the share of net worth held by the top 1 percent has more than doubled since 1976.

The 1998 high of 38.1 percent control of net worth by the top 1 percent was not an historic high, yet close to it. The historic high was in 1929—in an ominous time conjunction with the Great Depression. At that time the top 1 percent controlled just over 42 percent of the nation's privately-held net worth.

The severity of wealth concentration does not end with the top 1 percent. The next 4 percent of the wealthiest households controls an additional 23 percent of the nation's private net worth; the next wealthiest 5 percent of households controls an additional 12 percent. Taken together, the wealthiest 10 percent of households control 66 percent of the nation's private net worth. In 1998, before the recession and stock value drop, the top 10 percent of wealthholders controlled 70.9% of the nation's privately-held net worth. (Edward N. Wolff, "Recent Trends in Wealth Ownership, 1983-1998," plus updates.)

GRAPH 5

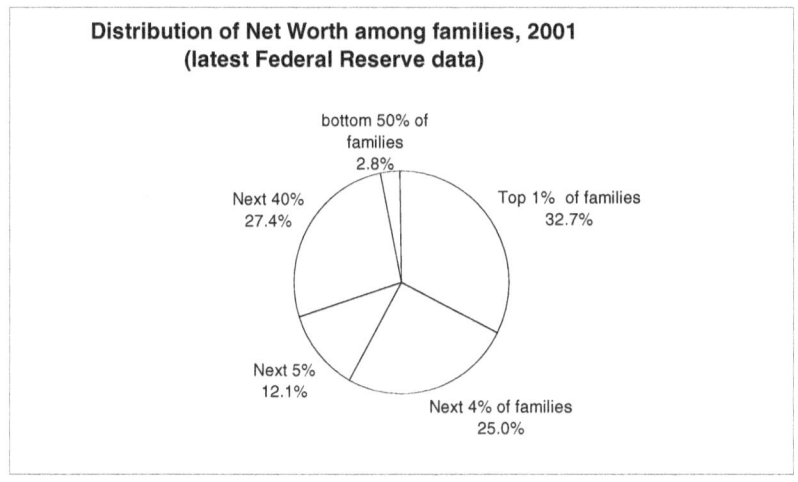

Financial wealth—stocks, bonds, and other financial securities—is even more concentrated in the hands of the rich than are other assets. The wealthiest 10 percent of families owns about 85 percent of all stocks and other financial securities. They own 90 percent of all business assets.

TABLE 3, below, shows the distribution of net worth by selected groups:

Average Family net worth by wealth class: 2001: (2001 dollars)
(2001 is the year of the latest Federal Reserve Board data.)

		Ratio of top 10% to bottom 40%
Bottom 25% of wealthholders.........	zero	501 to 1
Bottom 40%...............	* $ 5,500	
		Ratio of top 1% to bottom 40%
Next 25-49.9%	$ 44,100	
Next 50-74.9%	$ 165,700	
Next 75-89.9%	$ 449,400	2429 to 1
Next 90-100%	$ 2,754,900	
Top 1%	* $ 13,361,300	

(Sources: Ana M. Aizcorbe, Arthur B. Kennickell, Kevin B. Moore, Federal Reserve Board, Division of
Research and Statistics, Recent Changes in U.S. Family Finances: Evidence from the 1998 and 2001
Survey of Consumer Finances. Also, Edward N Wolff, Recent Trends in Wealth Ownership, 1983
to 1998. * Approximate figure extrapolated from Edward Woff data.
** Approximate figure extrapolated from Edward N. Wolf study "Recent
Trends... " and Federal Reserve data.)

The Racial and Hispanic Gap in Wealth:

The average black household controls about 12.5% the wealth of the average white/non-Hispanic household.

The average black household controls about 3.1% of the *financial* wealth of the average white/non-Hispanic family.

The average Hispanic household controls 3.7% the wealth of the average white/non-Hispanic household.

(Source: Edward N. Wolff, "Recent Trends in Wealth Ownership, 1983-1998," plus updates.)

Net Worth of Households, Select Groups, 2003:

The bottom 20% of all households have, on average, zero net worth.

The bottom 15% of all white households have, on average, zero net worth.

The bottom 29% of all black households have, on average, zero net worth.

100% of Hispanic households, averaged together, have zero net worth.

A Federal Reserve survey found that 40 percent of families headed by persons 25 to 54 years of age had no savings whatever.

The GINI index for wealth concentration in the U. S. is .82. As a practical matter, it is almost impossible to reach higher levels of concentration.

The degree of wealth concentration in the U.S. is three times higher than that of the industrialized nation with the second-highest concentration (Germany).

References

Poverty and Personal and Family Responsibility:

[1] Patrick Fagan, Stephanie Coontz, "Q: Are single-parent families a major cause of social dysfunction?" Symposium paper presented in "Insight in the News," Dec 8, 1997, v.13 n45 p24.

[2] The Fagan, Coontz dollar values have been adjusted to 2003 dollars. The numerical relationship expressed in their findings have not changed significantly.

[3] National Commission on the Causes and Prevention of Violence, year 2000 study update by the Milton S. Eisenhower Foundation, cited in William F. Buckley Jr. Article, National Review, New York, Feb. 7, 2000.

[4] David J. Eggebeen and Daniel T. Lichter, "Race, Family Structure, and Changing Poverty Among American Children," American Sociological Review, n56, Dec. 1991.

[5] S.S. McLanahan, "The Consequences of Single Motherhood," The American Prospect, v18, 1994. Also; Patrick F. Fagan, "How Broken Families Rob Children of their Chances for Future Prosperity," Heritage Foundation, Backgrounder No. 1283, June 11, 1999.

[6] Suzanne Bianchi and Edith McArthur, Family Disruption and Economic Hardship, U. S. Census Bureau, 1991.

[7] Sara McLanahan and Gary Sandefur, Growing Up with a Single Parent: What Hurts, What Helps, Harvard University Press, Cambridge, Mass., 1994.

Poverty and Crime:

[1] Males, M., e-published essay, http://www.fair.org/extra/9603/teen violence, html.

2 Loftin and Hill (1974); Flango and Sherbenou (1976); Parker and Smith (1979); Smith and Parker (1980); Parker and Loftin (1983); Williams, 1984.

3 Steven Raphael and Rudolf Winter-Ebmer, "Identifying the Effects of Unemployment on Crime, Goldman School of Public Policy, University of California, Berkley and Dept. of Economics, University of Linz, Austria, 1999, revised, 2000; see their survey of literature.

4 Freeman, R. (1996), "Why Do So Many Young American Men Commit Crimes and What Might We Do About It?" Journal of Economic Perspectives, 10(1):25-42, Winter edition.

5 Bound, John and Richard B. Freeman (1992), "What Went Wrong? The Erosion of Relative Earnings and Employment Among Young Black Men in the 1980s," Quarterly Journal of Economics 107,201-231; also, Grogger, Jeff (1995), "The Effect of Arrest on the Employment and Earnings of Young Men," Quarterly Journal of Economics 110, 51-72; also, Nagin, Daniel and Joel Waldfogel (1995), "The Effects of Criminality and Conviction on the Labor Market Status of Young British Offenders," International Review of Law and Economics 15, 109-126.

6 Imrohoroglu, A., Merlow, A., and Rupert, P. (2000), "What Accounts for the Decline in Crime," Working Paper 0008, Federal Reserve Bank of Cleveland.

7 Grogger J. (1998), "Market Wages and Youth Crime," Journal of Labor Economics, v16, 756-91; also, Witte, A. D., and H. Tauchen (1994), "Work and crime: An exploration using panel data." Public Finance, v49, pp 155-167.

8 The Honorable William P. Barr, "Crime Poverty and the Family," Heritage Lecture #401, The Heritage Foundaton, 1992.

9 Ibid., The Honorable William P. Barr.

10 Ibid., The Honorable William P. Barr, citing June O'Neill, formerly of the Urban Institute.

11 Harper, Cynthia and Sara S. McLanahan, "Father Absence and Youth Incarceration," paper presented to the American Sociological Association, San Francisco, 1998; (data tabulated for this report ending in 1996).

[12] Elder, G. H. Jr., T. Van Nguyen, and A. Caspi (1985), "Linking Family Hardship to Children's Lives," Child Development, vol. 56. Pp. 361-75. Larzelere, R. E., and G. R. Patterson (1990), "Parental Management: Mediator of the effect of socioeconomic status on early delinquency," Criminology, vol. 28, no. 2, pp. 301-23. Harris, K. M. and J. K. Marmer (1996), "Poverty, Paternal Involvement, and Adolescent Well-being," Journal of Family Issues, vol. 17, no. 5, pp. 614-40.

[13] Loeber R. and M. Stothhamer-Loeber (1986), "Family Factors as Correlates and Predictors of Juvenile Conduct Problems and Delinquency," Crime and Justice: An annual review of research, vol. 7, eds M. Tonry and N. Morris, University of Chicago Press, Chicago, pp. 29-149. Widom, C. S. (1989), "Child Abuse, Neglect, and Violent Criminal Behavior," Criminology, vol. 27, no. 2, pp. 251-71. Larzelere, R. E., and G. R. Patterson (1990), "Parental Management: Mediator of the effect of socioeconomic status on early delinquency," Criminology, vol. 28, no. 2, pp. 301-23. Thornberry, T. P., Lizotte, A. J., Krohn, M. D., Farnworth, M., and Jang, S. J. (1991). "Testing Interactional Theory: An examination of reciprocal causal relationships among family, school, and delinquency," Rochester Youth Development Study, The Journal of Criminal Law and Criminology, vol. 82, no. 1, pp 3-33. Barnes, G. M. and Ferrell, M. P. (1992), "Parental Support and Control as Predictors of Adolescent Drinking, Delinquency, and Related Problem Behaviors," Journal of Marriage and Family, vol. 54, pp.763-76. Martens, P. (1992), "Family, Environment and Delinquency," National Council for Crime Prevention, Stockholm, Sweden. Mak, A. S. (1994), "Parental Neglect and Overprotection as Risk Factors in Delinquency," Australian Journal of Psychology, vol. 46, no. 2, pp. 107-111. Smith, C. and Thornberry, T. P. (1995), "The Relationship Between Childhood Maltreatment and Adolescent Involvement in Delinquency," Criminology, vol. 33, no. 4, pp. 451-81.

[14] U.S. Dept of Health and Human Services, Administration for Children and Families, "A Nation's Shame: Fatal Child Abuse and Neglect in the U.S., Fifth Report," United States Advisory Board on Child Abuse and Neglect, 1995.

[15] U.S. Dept. of Health and Human Resources, The National Center on Child Abuse and Neglect, U.S., Reports NIS-1, 1980; NIS-2, 1986; NIS-3, 1993; released: Sept, 1996.

[16] Pelton, L.H. (1985) The Social Context of Child Abuse and Neglect. New York: Human Science Press, Inc.; and Wollock, I., and Horowitz, B. (1979) Child Maltreatment and Maternal Deprivation Among AFDC-recipient Families, Social Service Review, 53 (June), 175-194; and Wollock and Horowitz (1984) Child Maltreatment as a Social Problem: The neglect of neglect. American Journal of Orthopsychiatry, 54 (4), 530-543.

[17] Robert Whelan, "Broken Homes and Battered Children: a study of the relationship between child abuse and family type," Family Education Trust, London, 1993.

[18] Gil, 1970; Gelles, 1973; Parke and Collmer, 1975; Madden and Wrench, 1977; Pelton, 1978; Burgdorf, 1980; National Center on Child Abuse and Neglect, 1988.

[19] Peter C. Kratcoski, "Families Who Kill," Marriage and Family Review, Vol. 12, No. 1-2 (1987), pp. 47-70.

[20] D.O. Lewis, J. H. Pincus, B. Bard, E. Richardson, L. S. Prichep, M. Feldman, and C. Yager, "Neuropsychiatric, Psychoeducational and Family Characteristics of 14 Juveniles Condemned to Death in the United States," American Journal of Psychiatry, Vol.145 (1988), pp. 585-589.

[21] C. M. Mouzakitis, "An Inquiry into Child Abuse and Juvenile Delinquency," in R. J. Hunner and Y. E. Walker, eds., Exploring the Relationship Between Child Abuse and Delinquency (Montclair, N. J.: Osmun and Allanheld, 1981). Also see P.W. Rhodes and S. L. Parker, "The Connections Between Youth Problems and Violence in the Home," Oregon Coalition Against Domestic and Sexual Violence, Portland, ore., 1981.

[22] "The Cycle of Violence," National Institute of Justice, October, 1992.

[23] "Violence by intimates: Analysis of Data on Crimes by Current or Former Spouses, Boyfriends, and Girlfriends," U.S. Dept of Justice, Special Report, March, 1998.

[24] Uniform Crime Reports of the U.S., Federal Bureau of Investigation, 1996.

[25] This range of incidence reflects survey results over the last ten years using various definitions and data collection methods. It is heartening that almost all categories of violence against women have seen meaningful reductions

since 1993. Not so heartening is that research confirms that violence against women, particularly violence within marriages and rape, is substantially underreported. This spread reflects different definitions and different sampling methods: the lower incidence (7.7 per 1000) is based on a survey that attempts to identify criminal behavior. It is based on a broad population, inclusive of all women aged twelve and over—not just women of marriageable age or those who might consider cohabitation with an intimate partner. The higher incidence (116 per 1000) derives from a broad definition of violence, including threats and other psychological abuse. The base population of this survey is 'couples—either married or cohabiting, thereby largely excluding women from age twelve to eighteen.

26 M. A. Allard, R. Albelda, M. E. Colton and C. Cosenza, "In Harm's Way: Domestic violence, AFDC receipt, and welfare reform in Massachusetts," a report from the University of Massachusetts, McCormick Institute, Boston, 1997.

27 C. Curio, The Passaic County study of AFDC recipients in a welfare-to-work program, for Passaic County Board of Social Services, Passaic County, New Jersey, 1997.

28 A. Saloman, S. Bussuk and M. Brooks, "Patterns of welfare use among poor and homeless women," American Journal of Orthopsychiatry v66 pp510-525.

29 S. Lloyd, The Effects of Violence on Women's Employment, report from the Institute for Policy Research, Northwestern University.

30 J. Raphael and R. Tolman, Trapped by Poverty/Trapped by Abuse: New evidence documenting the relationship between domestic violence and welfare. From the Project for Research on Welfare, Work, and Domestic Violence: a collaboration between Taylor Institute and the University of Michigan (1997). Also, J. Raphael, "Domestic Violence and Welfare Receipt: The unexplored barrier to employment," Georgetown Journal on Fighting Poverty III: pp. 29-34.

31 R. Tolman and J. Raphael, "A Review of Research on Welfare and Domestic Violence," Journal of Social Issues, v 56, n 4, pp. 655-682, 2000.

32 "Violence Against Women: A National Crime Victimization Survey Report," U.S. Department of Justice, Washington, D.C., Jan. 1994.

[33] K. D. O'Leary, J. Malone, A. Tyree, "Physical Aggression in Early Marriage: pre-relationship and relationship effects," Journal of Consulting Clinical Psychology, v 62, pp. 594-602, 1994.

[34] "Intimate-partner Violence," Bureau of Justice Statistics, special report, NCJ 178247, May, 2000.

[35] E. Gondorf, E. Fisher, "Battered Women as Survivors: An alternative to treating learned helplessness," Lexington, MA., 1988.

[36] "Report of the American Psychological Association Presidential Task Force on Violence and the Family, 1996."

Poverty and Health:

[1] McDonough, P., Duncan, G.J., Williams, D., House, J.S., "Income Dynamics and Adult Maturity in the U.S. from 1972 through 1989"; American Journal of Public Health, 1997;87:1476-1483.

[2] Lynch, J.W., Kaplan G.A., Pamuk, E.R., Cohen, R.D., Heck, K.E.,Balfour, J.L., and Yen, I.H.; "Income inequality and mortality in metropolitan areas of the United States," American Journal of Public Health, Vol. 88, Issue 7 1074-1080, 1998.

[3] Davey-Smith, G.; Hart, G.; Hole, D.; Hawthorn, V.; "Individual social class, area-based deprivation, cardiovascular disease risk factors, and mortality: the Renfrew and Paisley Study." Journal of Epidemiol Community Health, 1998; 52:399-405.

[4] Carstairs, V.; "Deprivation indices: their interpretation and use in relation to health," Journal of Epidemiol Community Health, 1955; 49 (sup.2):S3-8.

[5] Davey-Smith, G.; Dorling, D.; "I'm all right, John": voting patterns and mortality in England and Wales, 1981-1992; British Medical Journal, 313:1573-7, 1995.

[6] Davey-Smith, G.; Neaton, J.D.; Wentworth, D.; Stamler, J.; "Socioeconomic differentials in mortality risk among men screened for the multiple risk factors interventional trial," American Journal of Public Health, 86:486-96, 1996.

7 The Children's Defense Fund has several studies that review the literature on infant mortality. Infant mortality data can be found on the National Center for Health Statistics website.

8 Center for Disease Control, 2000 report.

9 The 70 percent chance of survival until sixty-five years of age for white males was extrapolated from mortality tables. The 37 percent chance of survival to age sixty-five for black males living in Harlem was calculated by University of Michigan researchers Geronimus, Arline T., et al, "Excess mortality among blacks and whites in the United States," The New England Journal of Medicine 335 (21), November 21, 1996.

10 Geronimus, A., Bound, J., Waidmann, T., Colen, C., Steffick, D., "Inequality in life expectancy, functional status, and active life expectancy across selected black and white populations in the United States," Demography; May, 2001.

11 Almgren, G., Guest, A., Immerwahr, G., Spittel, M., "Joblessness, family disruption, and violent death in Chicago, 1970-1990," Social Forces, June, 1998.

12 Ibid. Almgren, et al.

13 Kahn, R.S., Wise, P.H., Kennedy, B.P., Kawachi, I., "State income inequality, household income, and maternal mental health and physical health: cross-sectional national survey," British Medical Journal, Nov. 25, 2000, v321;7272 p 1311.

14 Kennedy, B.D., Kawachi, I., Glass, R., Prothrow-Stith, D., "Income distribution, socioeconomic status, and self-reported health in the U.S.: Multilevel analysis," British Medical Journal, 1998; 317:917-91.

The Total Dollar-cost of Poverty in the United States:

1 First an estimate for the overall cost of crime must be made; then an estimate of the percentage attributable to poverty must be made. To estimate the overall cost of crime is not simple. To approach it with precision is extremely costly because of the necessary breadth of research. Consequently, few comprehensive studies have been attempted. Four studies that attempted to put a comprehensive cost on crime were discovered. A 1967 study by the President's Commission on Law Enforcement; a 1974 attempt by U.S. News magazine researchers; a

1994 study by Cohen, Miller and Rossman; a 1999 study by David A. Anderson. All of these studies can be criticized on various grounds. However, when adjusted for missing components (primarily "opportunity costs") and inflation rates for criminal justice expenditures, there is surprising continuity among them. They show a progression of cost generally reflecting incarceration rates: 1967= $737 billion; 1974 = $998 billion; 1994= $1.05 trillion; 1997= $1.26 trillion. All these values are in 2003 dollars. The average value of these studies for the overall cost of crime in 2003 dollars was $1.01 trillion. Bear in mind that these are approximations; plus or minus 100 billion is the probable range of error.

This study concludes that approximately 50 percent of the cost of all crime can be reasonably attributed to poverty. Great caution was exercised to assure that this was a conservative estimate. Numerous assumptions, estimates, and guesses were required. The following data is drawn from the U.S. Department of Justice, Bureau of Justice Statistics, unless otherwise noted. All data is year 2000 or later, unless otherwise noted.

Over 70 percent of inmates had served prior jail or prison sentences, or had been convicted and placed on probation. This infers substantial levels of repeat offender behavior or career criminal behavior, both of which are strongly correlated to the poverty culture and the underculture. A total of 272,111 offenders first discharged from prison in 1994 accounted for 4,877,000 subsequent arrests over their recorded criminal histories. That is an average of 17.9 arrests per criminal, These arrests of course reflect only those criminal episodes for which they were caught. Again, career criminality is almost exclusively the domain of the underculture, the reserve of the most severe and chronic poverty.

Sixty-four percent of prison inmates belong to minority groups, minority status being a strong proxy variable for poverty. The balance of prison inmates are mostly poor whites.

Between 82 and 96 percent of all state-prosecuted individuals (this range reflects differing results in different states) are legally indigent and must be provided public defenders. In a survey of the 75 largest U.S. Jurisdictions, 90 to 96 percent of defendants were indigent.

Forty-three percent of all state prison inmates did not graduate from high school, a strong correlate to low-income status.

Thirty-six percent of inmates were unemployed during the month before they were arrested. Sixteen percent were 'discouraged' members of the labor force, that is they were unemployed and had given up looking for work.

In a survey of twenty-four cities, 50 percent of all arrestees tested positive for recent drug use. About one-third were under the influence of drugs at the time of their arrest. Drug use during the commission of a crime is strongly correlated to low-income status.

Using race as a proxy variable for poverty (in the context of criminal studies, poverty and being black are overwhelmingly correlated) the incarceration rate for blacks is 7.7 times that for whites. If we were to assume that all black arrestees are poor, and all white arrestees are not poor, the rates suggest that about three of every four crimes are committed by poor people. But this understates the effect of poverty. Whereas it is substantially (but not entirely, of course) true that all black arrestees are low-income, it is also true that most white arrestees are also poor. This author could not find a statistic for the proportion of white arrestees who were poor, but we do know that overall 82 to 96 percent of those prosecuted are poor, suggesting that most white arrestees are also low-income.

Eighty percent of gunshot victims were on public assistance or without health insurance at this time of the shooting. Although violent crime represents only about 4.6 percent of all crime, violent crime generates almost 50 percent of all criminal justice related expenditures—primarily due to medical costs and the lost productivity of persons prematurely killed or disabled, as well as the high average cost of prosecuting these cases.

Again, this study concludes that approximately 50 percent of the total cost of crime in the United States can be justifiably attributed to poverty, or approximately $600 billion per year.

2 Cash and Non-cash Programs for Persons with Limited Income, FY2000-FY2002, Congressional Research Office.

3 Regarding "other non-means-tested transfer payments": Social Security alone keeps 49 percent of retirees out of poverty: that is, without Social Security just under half of all senior citizens would fall below the poverty line. Medicare saves many more seniors from the same fate. Even with Medicare, many seniors are but one major illness or injury away from poverty because of non-covered costs, co-pays, and drug coverage that will not apply until 2006, and then not at 100 percent. The Social Security program also covers many disability costs for adults and children who are eligible on criteria other than means-testing, but who nevertheless are poor. These cases are on a line item separate from Medicare or Medicaid. These programs are erroneously referred to as 'insurance'

programs; they are in fact pay-as-we-go. Again, about 50 percent of all Social Security payments effectively keep the elderly out of poverty, working, in effect, with the same object or intent as welfare programs. Fifty percent of all Social Security and Medicare expenditures are regarded as poverty-associated.

100 percent of Medicaid is attributed to poverty.

100 percent of all Supplemental Security Income, Family Assistance, Food Stamps, and other miscellaneous income maintenance programs are associated with poverty.

50 percent of federal education and training assistance is estimated to be associated with poverty.

25 percent of 'other payments to individuals' is estimated to be associated with poverty.

No unemployment insurance benefits were attributed to poverty, nor were any veterans benefit payments attributed to poverty. However, both of these programs serve 'supplemental income'/welfare roles in keeping large numbers of persons above the poverty line.

[4] Surveys conducted by, or reported by, Charity Choices. The 2001 survey was adjusted upward by 2.5 percent per annum to reflect 2003 giving rates for the social services. www.charitablechoices.org/chargive.asp.

[5] As reported in Health Care Financing and Organization (an on-line magazine), March, 2002. The amount reported was inflated by a medical cost inflator of 4.4 percent, the five-year average rate of inflation between 1998 and 2004.

[6] Nils, Christy, in a 2002 study put a cost of $115 billion for private security; Anderson, David, 1999, specified a cost of $46 billion for private security. The average is $83.8 billion after adjustment to 2003 dollars. The author assumes 50 percent of crime overall is attributable to poverty and its culture. That yields a figure of $41.9 billion.

[7] 2001 Urban League study, inflated by CPI-U to 2003 dollars. The author estimates that 75 percent of these expenditures focus on low-income families, and families on welfare.

[8] Cohen, Mark A.; Wiersema, Brian; Victim Costs and Consequences: A new look, 1996. Cohen and Wiersema put a 1995 cost on violent crime of about $426 billion. Using a criminal justice cost inflator of 6 percent yields a 2003 figure of $679 billion. This author estimates that conservatively, 75 percent of violent crime can be associated with low-income or

poverty status. That yields a 2003 cost for violent crime of 509.3 billion dollars.

[9] Anderson, David A., Journal of Law and Economics, XLII, Oct. 1999; Also Collins, 1994; Cohen, Miller, and Wiersema, 1995; Cohen, Miller, and Rossman, 1994. Some cost estimates were averaged between studies. Costs were updated to 2003 dollars using a conservative medical cost inflation rate of 8 percent.

[10] U.S. Department of Justice, Bureau of Justice Statistics, updated to 2003 based on adjustments for imprisonment rates and an criminal justice cost inflation rate of 6 percent per annum.

[11] National Association of Crime Victim Compensation Boards. Victim Compensation Quarterly. $1.89 billion in 2003. This compensation is almost entirely for violent crime victims. 50 percent is conservatively estimated to be associated with low-income and poverty status. That yields a figure of $95 billion in 2003 dollars.

[12] The Executive Office of the President through the Office of National Drug Policy commissioned The Levin Group to determine the national cost of drug abuse from 1992 through 1998, and to project costs through 2000. For year 2000 their estimate was $160.7 billion. They established a drug abuse cost inflator of 4.9 percent, reflecting mostly medical costs and criminal justice costs. Using that inflator, a 2003 dollar figure of $185.5 billion. This author estimates that at least 50 percent of this cost can be associated with poverty and its culture. This yields an estimated 2003 dollar-cost for poverty-related drug abuse in the U.S. of $92.8 billion..

[13] Based on above report.

[14] ibid.

[15] ibid.

[16] Data summarized by Prevent Child Abuse America in 2001. See PCAA website for full biography of supporting studies: www.preventchildabuse.org. This author estimates that 75 percent of child abuse is linked with low-income and welfare households.

[17] The Center for Disease control commissioned studies and reviewed existing studies to determine the cost of intimate partner abuse in 1995. These studies focused on health care and lost productivity. Criminal Justice costs were not included. The CDC, 1995 estimate was 5.8 billion dollars

in 1995, adjusted by a medical cost inflator of 4.4 percent, yields a value of $8.2 billion in 2003 dollars. The Bureau of Justice Statistics estimates the criminal justice component of intimate partner abuse to be about 15 percent of all direct crime costs in the U.S. That would be 15 percent of about $120.5 billion in 2003, or about $18 billion. That suggests a total cost of approximately $26.2 billion in 2003 dollars. The incidence of intimate partner abuse is has been found to be three to ten time higher in low income groups, depending on how the group is defined. This author estimates, for this purpose, that 75 percent of the cost of intimate partner abuse attaches to low-income or poverty status. That would put the figure at $19.9 billion in 2003 dollars.

[18] National Association of Insurers. Adjusted to 2003 dollars. 50 percent of payouts have been attributed to poverty and its culture. That yields a figure of $22.5 billion.

[19] Bureau of Justice Statistics, Indigent Defense Statistics; data drawn from a 1999 study, inflated at 6 percent, reflecting the rate of cost increase for legal services. This value was cross-referenced to other BJS findings: that indigent defense costs average about 3 percent of all local (county and city) criminal justice expenditures.

About the Author

Mr. Berg has taught Political Science and Economics in various colleges over the past fifteen years.

In his varied career, he has worked in industry, owned his own business, served as Assistant Dean of Students at a college in Nebraska, served as Assistant to the Chancellor for Student Relations at the University of Nebraska, worked as an Area Campaign Director for Rep. John Y. McCollister (2nd District, Nebraska), and as a Legislative Aid for State Senator Vard Johnson, (8th District, Nebraska). Mr. Berg, not knowing better, once ran for a seat in the Nebraska State Senate. (Soundly trounced.)

He gave up politics for teaching and made a career of it. He now presumes that he can write.

He is married to Leigh Anderson. They have two daughters, Andrea 11, and Emily 7. They live on Whidbey Island, in Washington state.

0-595-31948-3